TRAVERSE
THEATRE

SCOTLAND'S NEW WRITING THEATRE

Traverse Theatre Company

In the Bag

by Wang Xiaoli

in a version by Ronan O'Donnell
literal translation by cris bevir

Man	Daniel York
Woman	Tuyet Le
Younger Brother	Mo Zainal
Wife	Michelle Macerlean

Director	Lorne Campbell
Designer	Jon Bausor
Lighting Designer	Philip Gladwell
Sound Designer	DJRed6
Script Associate	Katherine Mendelsohn
Voice Coach	Ros Steen
Stage Manager	Lee Davis
Deputy Stage Manager	Alison Brodie
Assistant Stage Manager	Kenna Grant
Wardrobe Supervisor	Aileen Sherry
Video Projection	Peter Anderson

**First performed at the Traverse Theatre,
Edinburgh, on Friday 29 April 2005**

TRAVERSE THEATRE

Powerhouse of new writing   DAILY TELEGRAPH

Artistic Director Philip Howard

The Traverse is Scotland's new writing theatre. Founded in 1963 by a group of maverick artists and enthusiasts, it began as an imaginative attempt to capture the spirit of adventure and experimentation of the Edinburgh Festival all year round. Throughout the decades, the Traverse has evolved and grown in artistic output and ambition. It has refined its mission by strengthening its commitment to producing new plays by Scottish and international playwrights and actively nurturing them throughout their careers. Traverse productions have been seen worldwide and tour regularly throughout the UK and overseas.

The Traverse has produced over 600 new plays in its lifetime and, through a spirit of innovation and risk-taking, has launched the careers of many of the country's best known writers. From, among others, Stanley Eveling in the 1960s, John Byrne in the 1970s, Liz Lochhead in the 1980s, to David Greig and David Harrower in the 1990s, the Traverse is unique in Scotland in its dedication to new writing. It fulfils the crucial role of providing the infrastructure, professional support and expertise to ensure the development of a dynamic theatre culture for Scotland.

The Traverse's activities encompass every aspect of playwriting and production, providing and facilitating play reading panels, script development workshops, rehearsed readings, public playwriting workshops, writers' groups, discussions and special events. The Traverse's work with young people is of supreme importance and takes the form of encouraging playwriting through its flagship education project *Class Act*, as well as the Traverse Young Writers' Group. In 2004, the Traverse took the Class Act project to Russia and also staged *Articulate*, a pilot project with West Dunbartonshire Council for 11 to 14 year olds.

Edinburgh's Traverse Theatre is a mini-festival in itself   THE TIMES

From its conception in the 1960s, the Traverse has remained a pivotal venue during the Edinburgh Festival. It receives enormous critical and audience acclaim for its programming, as well as regularly winning awards. In 2002 the Traverse produced award-winning shows, *Outlying Islands* by David Greig and *Iron* by Rona Munro and in 2003, *The People Next Door* by Henry Adam picked up Fringe First and Herald Angel awards before transferring to the Theatre Royal, Stratford East. Re-cast and with a new director, *The People Next Door* has since toured to Germany and the Balkans. In 2004, the Traverse produced the award-winning *Shimmer* by Linda McLean and a stage adaptation of Raja Shehadeh's diary account of the Israeli occupation of Ramallah, *When The Bulbul Stopped Singing*. This play won the Amnesty International Freedom of Expression Award 2004, appeared in January 2005 as part of the Fadjr International Theatre Festival in Tehran and toured to New York in Spring 2005.

For further information on the Traverse Theatre's activities and history, an online resource is available at www.virtualtraverse.co.uk. To find out about ways to support the Traverse, please contact Norman MacLeod, Development Manager on 0131 228 3223.

www.traverse.co.uk • www.virtualtraverse.co.uk

THE JOURNEY TO STAGING 'IN THE BAG'

by Katherine Mendelsohn
Literary Manager, Traverse Theatre

It's been an extraordinary journey getting this play to the stage. What we started in late 2001 has taken almost four years to get onto the stage here: the first ever British production of a contemporary play from mainland China.

Back in 2001 the Traverse had already undertaken several of its *Playwrights in Partnership* play commissions, where we find contemporary international plays we want to put on our stages, and then match the playwright with a Scottish writer who can recreate the play's life-breath in a different language. Stephen Greenhorn had worked with Belgian playwright Arne Sierens, Linda McLean with Finnish writer Laura Ruohonen, David Harrower was being paired with Jon Fosse from Norway, and Isabel Wright with François Archambault from Québec. From this early work with playwrights from Europe and Québec (Canada), we were keen to take a step further and go on to explore work from countries further afield like those in Asia.

Apart from in the financial pages, in 2001 the very few British news stories there were about China were most often clichés about peasants in rice-fields, or at the other extreme about politics. Contemporary, urban Chinese life was less evident. But in the cultural world we'd seen some great contemporary films starting to emerge from China, and for me that is something that often signals a possibly interesting presence of new writing for the stage in a country. Really fresh new plays from China were then off our radar in Britain – almost impossible to access at the time because of the language barrier and the lack of translations or theatrical exchange between our two countries. I didn't even know if new writing for theatre was happening in China in the same way, or what the writer's status in theatre was, but I was keen to find out and to look at new Chinese plays.

What had limited those few British theatre practitioners making visits to China at the time was often their lack of the language, making it hard to stray off any guided, beaten track. China is a huge country; unknown to most of us, and with a language we don't read, let alone speak. What we needed at the Traverse was someone to go out on our behalf. Someone fluent in Mandarin, who could talk to people in their own language and knew the customs of the country, and yet who also had a crucial grasp of the theatre world back here in Britain and what our needs might be. That person was Cris Bevir. Cris and I had worked together in London theatre in the past and had often talked of developing truly contemporary Chinese plays in Britain.

Thanks to grants we raised from both the Scottish Arts Council and the British Council in China, Cris spent several months in Beijing 'mapping' the state of new writing there for the Traverse: talking to playwrights, artistic directors, dramaturgs and venue managers; seeing new work in festivals, and reading new Chinese plays. Many of these plays followed more traditional Chinese story models: a scholar-hero on his journey to the city – the sort of genre which, whilst of some curiosity, tells us less of the contemporary life of the country. And then we found Wang Xiaoli's play IN THE BAG, and knew we wanted to work with it. Bang up-to-date, the play reflects the pressures of modern, urban life – a story of two couples who have plenty but feel empty.

After the research project we commissioned Cris to do a literal translation of the play for us. Full of notes and questions about Xiaoli's often ambiguous language, this literal translation was an invaluable starting point for truly getting in touch with the play. We then asked Edinburgh playwright Ronan O'Donnell to be Xiaoli's partner playwright, feeling that his textured and creative Scots-English would echo Xiaoli's rhythms and images. We all four met together, and Ronan, Cris and myself (as dramaturg) explored the play with Xiaoli, asking her endless questions about the sound and the pace of her language, about tone and emotion, humour and anger. We had to understand what was really going on behind some of her innocuous exchanges between the characters – so that Ronan could begin to hint at the subtext while he captured the text. This was definitely harder than the work we had done so far with European languages, as we couldn't go back to the original text unaccompanied to look at a word or a phrase. In the end, this was to be the first of two residencies for Xiaoli at the Traverse and in between, Ronan worked through four or five drafts of this deceptively simple play until we had a text that was ready for performance on the British stage.

IN THE BAG tells us about two couples' lives in a city in China, but like all the best drama it also illuminates our own lives and situations. The play reveals a life where things seem sorted and 'in the bag', but where the inhabitants are quietly suffocating from the bag that surrounds them – paralysed into inaction. There's the writer who insists on his artistic credentials but whose novel is barely started and never finished; the younger brother whose insanely hard-working success in the business world still doesn't give him any certainty in life; the wife who's drowning in a wealthy but empty existence at home; and the woman who can't quite leave her dead relationship with the writer and move on.

Finally, there is a character in Xiaoli's play – a friend of the two brothers – who seems almost insignificant and who we never see: yet 'the French guy' nags at the back of our minds. He left Paris for China after university because his radical student friends all went to work in their daddies' banks, while he still sought true revolution. A peripheral character, he demonstrates a particular outsider's cliché about China as a land of revolution and pure ideology. He arrives in China with a naïve expectation of this complex country and ends up emotionally crushed by the gap between his dreams and the reality. Eventually he leaves for a different corner of the world – and ends up dead in a bar in Brazil, perhaps still searching for something that eludes him. IN THE BAG often plays with expectations of China, whether from outsiders or those of the Chinese. Everyone seems to have something they want China to be.

So what has changed in the four years since we started the project? Wider Western interest in China is now on the increase. (Even as I write, the BBC are about to screen 'China Week', a series of TV and radio programmes on China, as part of a lead-up to the 2008 Beijing Olympics.) It's still a people/place about which most of us in Europe know relatively little, and British theatre certainly still has an awful lot to explore. But by starting with Wang Xiaoli and her drama snapshot of the stories of four individuals in Beijing, at least we make a step towards finding out the modern-day reality beyond the clichés of the past.

March 2005

THE RESEARCH PROJECT

by cris bevir

Literal Translator of IN THE BAG

For me, going to Beijing in 2001 to do research for the Traverse Theatre's contemporary Chinese plays project was the culmination of ten years of work and study. My 'preparation' for the research trip had included studying Chinese at London University's School of Oriental and African Studies (SOAS), several year-long stays in China and Taiwan (Beijing, Shenzhen, Hong Kong and Taipei), and four years freelancing in the theatre industry in London.

Traditional Chinese opera is what first comes to mind, for many people in the UK, on hearing the words 'Chinese theatre'. Most imagine that Chinese theatre is Beijing Opera, the style of traditional theatre popularised by films like FAREWELL MY CONCUBINE. But at SOAS, I studied hua ju, or spoken theatre – the kind of Chinese theatre drawing on many of the same ancient and modern roots as theatre here, with no singing, no martial arts, no acrobatics. A style of theatre many people, even theatre practitioners, in the UK are surprised to hear exists. I knew there was a wealth of theatre in China with a close affinity to, and parallels with, the work staged by British theatres. None of it, however, was making its way to the UK.

There have been a few contemporary Chinese plays produced in the UK in the past fifteen years, but they have always been pro-duced in Chinese (with sub-titles) as part of international festivals: Zhang Yuan and Wang Xiaobo's EAST PALACE, WEST PALACE, which was performed as part of the Edinburgh International Festival in 1997, or the selection of work by directors from China in the London International Festival of Theatre also in 1997. There have also been some readings of contemporary plays in translation, again usually as part of festivals celebrating Chinese culture, such as Gao Xingjian's THE BUS STOP which was read at Manchester's Royal Exchange Theatre for the Spring Festival celebrations in 2001, and a second play by Gao Xingjian read as part of Yellow Earth's Typhoon III festival in 2004.

In 2001, I arrived in Beijing with two contacts: Rachel Henson, who was then working as Arts Manager at the British Council offices; and Luo Dajun, now Literary Manager of China's first National Theatre, who Katherine Mendelsohn (the Traverse

Theatre's Literary Manager) had met on a work trip in Israel.
Through them I came into contact with most of the theatre
practitioners working in Beijing.

A one-month stay became a four-month stay. I interviewed writers,
directors, actors, literary managers, artistic directors, producers,
translators, drama teachers, drama students, drama publishers,
and theatre scholars, asking them what were the good plays they
had seen recently.

We met in cafés and restaurants, sometimes after theatre
performances we had attended together, more often during the
work day. We also met at the opening of art shows, in bars, at
experimental film showings. Meetings were arranged not more
than two days in advance, if not on the same day. One contact
led me to another, and each interview added to the information
that I used to hone a list of playwrights.

After I returned from Beijing, the Traverse commissioned a full
translation of Wang Xiaoli's play IN THE BAG on the strength of
the reports and some partial translations I prepared on the plays.
Our aim of a new Chinese play in a mainstream British theatre
has been accomplished, and, I hope, will take the presentation
of contemporary theatre from China in the UK to a new level.

March 2005

THE WRITERS

Wang Xiaoli

Wang Xiaoli lives in Shunyi, on the outskirts of Beijing. A former journalist, Xiaoli trained in Dramatic Literature at Central Academy of Drama in Beijing and has written for television, film and theatre. Previous plays include: UNDER A STREET LIGHT (performed as a rehearsed reading at the Royal Court, London in 2004) and I LOVE XXX (performed at Abandoned Theatre, Beijing and toured to Tiny Alice Theatre, Tokyo in 1994). Recent projects include the screenplay, RETURN IN WINTER, for film director Shi Runjiu and A RIVAL SHOW, a new play about the mental-health system in contemporary Beijing. Xiaoli is currently working on a full-length play about a Chinese woman living in London. IN THE BAG was first produced in 2001 by Lin Zhaohua's Workshop and performed in the same year at the People's Art Theatre Studio, Beijing.

Ronan O'Donnell

Ronan O'Donnell lives in Edinburgh. Previous plays include THE CHIC NERDS (Traverse), BRAZIL (Theatre of Imagination), SPAMBAM (LookOut Theatre Company) and LYSISTRATA (Common Force Community Theatre). Ronan has just completed THE DOLL TOWER, a play based on the life of T E Lawrence and his Scottish bodyguard John Bruce for LLT/Unity Theatre, and is currently writing THE NED'S LAMENT for Common Force Community Theatre.

cris bevir
(Literal Translator)

cris bevir studied for a BA in Chinese (Modern and Classical) at the School of Oriental and African Studies (SOAS), London University, and lived in China during the nineties. She has worked with new writing in London since 1998.

In 1999, when she was working as New Writing Associate with Mu-Lan Theatre Company, she directed the Mu-Lan Festival of New Writing – the first UK festival of British East Asian writing. After completing an MA Anthropology of Media (East Asian Film and Theatre) at SOAS in 2001 she began her research into New Writing for Theatre in China with the Traverse. In 2003 she was commissioned by LIFT (London International Festival of Theatre) to investigate the impact of international theatre on London audiences.

COMPANY BIOGRAPHIES

Peter Anderson (Video Projection) A director in television and a video artist working in the theatre and with dance. Specialising in movement and dance on screen for over 20 years, recent credits include: BOY, GREENMAN and INFANTA (created over five years with choreographer Rosemary Lee for broadcast on BBC2); BRINK, PASSAGE (Queen Elizabeth Hall, London); DANCING NATION (Millennium Commission for the Foundation for Community Dance, UK). Peter is currently collaborating with Cathy Marston, associate choreographer at the Royal Opera House, on film projections for a dance adaptation of Ibsen's GHOSTS, due to be premiered at The Linbury Theatre, ROH, London in September 2005.

Jon Bausor (Designer) Trained: Exeter College of Art and Motley Theatre Design Course. Designs for theatre include: THE LAST WALTZ SEASON (Oxford Stage Company/Arcola Theatre); FRANKENSTEIN (Derby Playhouse); BREAD AND BUTTER (Tricycle Theatre); SANCTUARY, THE TEMPEST (Royal National Theatre); WINNERS, INTERIOR, THE EXCEPTION AND THE RULE, THE NEW TENANT, THE SOUL OF CHIEN-NU LEAVES HER BODY (Young Vic); THE TAMING OF THE SHREW (Theatre Royal Plymouth/Thelma Holt Ltd national tour); TARTUFFE, GHOSTS IN THE COTTONWOODS (Arcola); THE AMERICA PLAY (RADA); SWITCHBACK, POSSIBLE WORLDS (Tron Theatre); THE TEMPEST, WHAT THE WOMEN DID (Southwark Playhouse). Designs for dance include: BEFORE THE TEMPEST . . . AFTER THE STORM, SOPHIE/STATELESS (Linbury, Royal Opera House); MIXTURES (ENB/ Westminster Abbey); NON EXEUNT (Ballet Boyz/ Sadlers Wells). Design for Opera include: THE QUEEN OF SPADES (Edinburgh Festival Theatre); COSI FAN TUTTI (Handmade Opera) and KING ARTHUR (New Chamber Opera). Forthcoming work includes: THE KNOT GARDEN (Klangbogen Festival, Vienna); CYMBELINE (Regent's Park) and GHOSTS (Linbury, Royal Opera House).

Lorne Campbell (Director) Trained: Channel 4 Theatre Director's Scheme, RSAMD and Liverpool John Moores. Lorne joined the Traverse in 2002 and since then has been Director on THE NEST and Assistant Director on DARK EARTH, OUTLYING ISLANDS, MR PLACEBO, HOMERS and THE SLAB BOYS TRILOGY. Other theatre credits include: THE DUMB WAITER, DEATH AND THE MAIDEN, AN EVENING WITH DAMON RUNYON, A COMEDY OF ERRORS, AS YOU LIKE IT, JOURNEYS END (Forge Theatre); THE CHAIRS (RSAMD); THE CHEVIOT, THE STAG AND THE BLACK BLACK OIL (Taigh Chearsabhagh).

DJRed6 aka **Jonny Crawshaw (Sound Designer)** Edinburgh-based hip hop DJ, club promoter and music producer. DJs at monthly Saturday residency, Give It Some at the Bongo Club and plays with seven-piece hip hop soul jazz collective, Livesciences (www.livesciences. co.uk), monthly Fridays at Henry's Cellar Bar. Livesciences' debut album is due out in late spring, following last year's critically acclaimed single 'Heroes/Keep Your Science Live'. His first work for theatre, the sound design for IN THE BAG, features sourced tracks as well as original, new material from the band Livesciences.

Philip Gladwell (Lighting Designer) Theatre credits include: A WHISTLE IN THE DARK (Glasgow Citizens' Theatre); ALADDIN (Hackney Empire); HOT BOI! (Glasgow Citz and Soho Theatre); TAPE (Soho); BAD GIRLS (musical workshop for ATG); MOTHER COURAGE AND HER CHILDREN (Nottingham, Bristol, Ipswich); BREAD AND BUTTER (OSC); AWAKENING, ANOTHER FIRE: AMERICA (Push at Sadler's Wells); DREAMS FROM A SUMMERHOUSE (Watermill Theatre, Newbury); THE TEMPEST (Royal National Theatre); INTERIOR, WINNERS, THE EXCEPTION AND THE RULE, THE NEW TENNANT, WHEN THE WORLD WAS GREEN, A NIGHT AT THE CIRCUS, PANTHEON OF THE GODS, YOUNG HAMLET, THE SOUL OF CHIEN NU LEAVES HER BODY, STREETCAR TO TENNESSEE, PRIMARIES (Young Vic); WAY UP STREAM (Derby); MODERN LOVE (QEH); UNITE FOR THE FUTURE (Old Vic); DEAD FUNNY (Nottingham) and AN OPERATIC EVENING (Royal Opera House). Future productions include: THE MORRIS (Liverpool Everyman) and THE CANTERVILLE GHOST (Peacock Theatre).

Tuyet Le (*Woman*) Film credits include: TOMB RAIDER (Paramount); CODE 46 (BBC); LEMON CRUSH (E2 Films). Television credits include: ULTIMATE FORCE (ITV); THE BILL (Thames TV); SEE YOU SEE ME (BBC 2); TIME TRAVEL, GODS IN THE SKY (Channel 4).

Michelle Macerlean (*Wife*) Trained: The Poor School, London. Film credits include: LASKO (Lasko Films). Television credits include: ULTIMATE FORCE (ITV); GORY GREEK GODS (BBC).

Ros Steen (Voice/Dialect Coach): Trained at RSAMD. Has worked extensively in theatre, film and TV. For the Traverse: THE SLAB BOYS TRILOGY, DARK EARTH, HOMERS, OUTLYING ISLANDS, THE BALLAD OF CRAZY PAOLA, THE TRESTLE AT POPE LICK CREEK, HERITAGE (2001 and 1998), AMONG UNBROKEN HEARTS, SHETLAND SAGA, SOLEMN MASS FOR A FULL MOON IN SUMMER (as co-director), KING OF THE FIELDS, HIGHLAND SHORTS, FAMILY, KILL

THE OLD TORTURE THEIR YOUNG, THE CHIC NERDS, GRETA, LAZYBED, KNIVES IN HENS, PASSING PLACES, BONDAGERS, ROAD TO NIRVANA, SHARP SHORTS, MARISOL, GRACE IN AMERICA. Other theatre credits includes: TWELFTH NIGHT, DANCING AT LUGHNASA, DUCHESS OF MALFI, (Dundee Rep); BASH, DAMN JACOBITE BITCHES, OBSERVE THE SONS OF ULSTER MARCHING TOWARDS THE SOMME (Citizens' Theatre); WORD FOR WORD (Magnetic North); CAVE DWELLERS (7:84); EXILES (Jervis Young Directors/Young Vic); THE PRIME OF MISS JEAN BRODIE, PLAYBOY OF THE WESTERN WORLD (Royal Lyceum, Edinburgh). Film credits include: THE ADVENTURES OF GREYFRIARS BOBBY (Piccadilly Pictures); GREGORY'S TWO GIRLS (Channel Four Films). Television credits include: SEA OF SOULS, ROCKFACE, 2000 ACRES OF SKY (BBC).

Daniel York (Man) Theatre credits include: MADE IN ENGLAND (Firebrand Theatre Company); TARTUFFE (Basingstoke Haymarket); A FISH CALLED TAO (Spirit Dance UK); SUN IS SHINING, THE MAGIC FUNDOSHI, PORCELAIN (Mu-Lan Theatre Company); THE MERCHANT OF VENICE, THE COUNTRY WIFE, MOBY DICK (Royal Shakespeare Company). Film credits include: THE BEACH (Figment Films); ROGUE TRADER (Rogue Trader Productions); WHEN PEGGY SUE GOT MARRIED (Deco Films). Television credits include: WAKING THE DEAD, CASUALTY, CHAMBERS (BBC); THE BILL (ITV).

Mo Zainal (*Younger Brother*) Trained: Capitol Theatre, Manchester. Theatre credits include: PACIFIC OVERTURES (Donmar Warehouse); KING LEAR (Royal Shakespeare Company); HAMLET, KING JOHN, LOVE FOR LOVE (Capitol Theatre).

The commission of IN THE BAG was made possible by

from a research project in 2001 funded by

SPONSORSHIP

Sponsorship income enables the Traverse to commission and produce new plays and to offer audiences a diverse and exciting programme of events throughout the year. We would like to thank the following companies for their support:

CORPORATE SPONSORS

BBC Scotland

LUMISON

THE HALLION

Canon

NICHOLAS GROVES RAINES ARCHITECTS

ANNIVERSARY ANGELS

With thanks to

Claire Aitken of Royal Bank of Scotland for mentoring support
arranged through the Arts & Business Mentoring Scheme.
Purchase of the Traverse Box Office, computer network and
technical and training equipment has been made possible with
money from The Scottish Arts Council National Lottery Fund

The Traverse Theatre's work
would not be possible without the support of

The Traverse Theatre receives financial assistance from

The Calouste Gulbenkian Foundation, The Peggy Ramsay
Foundation, The Binks Trust, The Bulldog Prinsep Theatrical Fund,
The Esmée Fairbairn Foundation, The Gordon Fraser Charitable
Trust, The Garfield Weston Foundation, The Paul Hamlyn
Foundation, The Craignish Trust, Lindsay's Charitable Trust,
The Tay Charitable Trust, The Ernest Cook Trust, The Wellcome
Trust, The Sir John Fisher Foundation, The Ruben and Elisabeth
Rausing Trust, The Equity Trust Fund, The Cross Trust, N Smith
Charitable Settlement, Douglas Heath Eves Charitable Trust,
The Bill and Margaret Nicol Charitable Trust, The Emile Littler
Foundation, Mrs M Guido's Charitable Trust, Gouvernement du
Québec, The Canadian High Commission, The British Council,
The Daiwa Foundation, The Sasakawa Foundation,
The Japan Foundation

Charity No. SC002368

**Sets, props and costumes for
IN THE BAG**
created by Traverse Workshops
(funded by the National Lottery)

Scottish
Arts Council
LOTTERY FUNDED

Production photography by Douglas Robertson
Print photography by Laurence Winram

**For their continued generous support
of Traverse productions the Traverse thanks**

Habitat, Marks and Spencer, Princes Street
Camerabase, BHS, and Holmes Place

**For their help and support with this production of
IN THE BAG
the Traverse would like to thank:**

Nina Steiger and Soho Theatre for space to do a reading.

**Wang Xiaoli
would like to thank the following
for their support and assistance with this play:**

cris bevir, for introducing my play to the Traverse
and for doing the literal translation of IN THE BAG.

Lin Zhaohua, Director of the original production,
and the four actors in the original play –
Fang Bing, Tu Ling, Song Yang, Lin Xiyue –
Zhang Wu, the stage designer and Yuan Hong, the producer.

The British Council for their financial assistance for me
to visit the UK to collaborate with British theatre companies.

Katherine Mendelsohn and the Traverse Theatre
for choosing to produce IN THE BAG.

Nick Hern for choosing to publish IN THE BAG.

TRAVERSE THEATRE – THE COMPANY

IN THE BAG

by Wang Xiaoli

*Wang Xiaoli would like to dedicate
the play to Tim Murray*

in a version by Ronan O'Donnell

For Eileen

Characters

MAN, *ex-boyfriend of Woman, older brother of Younger Brother*

WOMAN, *ex-girlfriend of Man*

WIFE, *wife of Younger Brother*

YOUNGER BROTHER, *husband of Wife, younger brother of Man*

This text went to press before the end of rehearsals and may differ from the play as performed.

Scene One

Friday afternoon. In the descending lift of the office block where YOUNGER BROTHER *works. The lights in the lift flicker.*

WOMAN. So, how far have they got?

YOUNGER BROTHER. She's already sitting on his lap.

WOMAN. What else?

YOUNGER BROTHER. Is there any point you knowing the details?

WOMAN. I'm just curious.

YOUNGER BROTHER. You both had your moments. Leave it at that.

WOMAN. Do you think it has the makings?

YOUNGER BROTHER. You're about to get wed and you still care about him – classic!

WOMAN. He never talks about her. The younger model. She's a student. Studies French. Yesterday at work he calls me and asks if I'm available.

YOUNGER BROTHER. He called you?

WOMAN. He hasn't been to see his gran for ages, and wants me to visit with him.

YOUNGER BROTHER. What did you say?

WOMAN. I like the old lady. Always have. I guess he doesn't know I'm getting married.

YOUNGER BROTHER. Oh, I think he's got the message.

WOMAN. I don't know how. We're so scared to raise it. Walking on egg shells.

YOUNGER BROTHER (*his mobile rings*). Hold on. (*Answers mobile.*) I'm in the lift. Yeah, you can talk. I thought you said it was your safe time? I can't believe you missed the pill. Are you positive? Shit. How far gone? . . . I'll call you back in five minutes. (*He closes his mobile.*) This is not my day. Shit!

WOMAN. Was that your wife?

YOUNGER BROTHER. Yeah.

WOMAN. How can you talk to her like that?

YOUNGER BROTHER. Comes natural . . .

WOMAN. Now she'll be fuming.

YOUNGER BROTHER. . . . Pure instinct.

WOMAN. She's pregnant? That will give you plenty to worry about.

YOUNGER BROTHER. What would you know about being pregnant? With any luck you'll never have to face it.

WOMAN. If only.

Pause.

YOUNGER BROTHER. I don't feel I want a baby? Not yet. Should I?

WOMAN. It's not mine. It's a tough call.

YOUNGER BROTHER. Where you off to?

WOMAN. Back to the flat. To get my toothbrush. I don't like the idea of someone else using it. Makes my skin creep.

YOUNGER BROTHER. Read in the paper, this couple, squeezed the toothpaste tube in different places, got divorced after thirty years of nettle. Me? Personally I don't like women with long hair. It gets everywhere, on the carpet, bungs the plug hole . . .

WOMAN. So that's why your wife's hair is the exact same cut as yours. Now I know. Know something, you're the only couple left I admire. Everybody else is splitting up.

YOUNGER BROTHER. I've got to go back up. I've got a pile of files to get through. Personal Development crap.

WOMAN. You're always busy. Let's all go for a meal when you've time.

YOUNGER BROTHER. Ok.

WOMAN. I'll bring him along. Have you met him yet?

YOUNGER BROTHER. Who?

WOMAN. My future spouse – stupid.

YOUNGER BROTHER. Sorry. My mind's elsewhere. (*Sighs.*) You know the old saying about the cook?

WOMAN. Pardon?

YOUNGER BROTHER. 'Love and confusion, they taste the same and everybody must eat.'

WOMAN. Ciao.

WOMAN *exits.*

YOUNGER BROTHER. Ciao.

Scene Two

Later on Friday afternoon. Formula One is on TV. Magazines and newspapers are lying about.

WOMAN. Why do you like motor racing?

MAN. Who says I like it?

Pause.

WOMAN. Why do you like motor racing?

MAN. Who says I like it?

Laughs.

In between your teeth . . . there. There's something stuck.

WOMAN. Is it gone?

MAN. No, it's still there. Here, I'll help you.

WOMAN. I can manage myself.

MAN. There are some CDs I can't find. I made a list.

WOMAN. I borrowed them. I'm doing a feature in the next issue about new lyrics.

MAN. Mind and bring them back then . . . You got today's newspaper? (*She gives him the paper.*) This isn't news. It's got squat all to do with anything. Mingle-mangle bullshit. And check the extremely complicated weather report. I mean, check it out. It's not like we live in the UK or anything. Ah, the book reviews. What a waste of ink. Substandard drivel, moral autism to the fore, pernicious. What can you say? The Ministry of Circumlocution rules, ok! How NOT to write!

WOMAN. You write something then.

MAN. Why would they want me when they have droners queuing round the block? Droners with qualifications – long as your arm. Hey, have you pinched that novel again? I'm halfway through it.

WOMAN. It's mine. Research material.

MAN. It was me told you to buy it. Research material? See, I said it would come in handy. (*Throws down the newspaper.*) Even my mum's cat could write for that lot. Six thousand words on cat flaps. How hard is it to get published? No bother if it's some feeble human-interest angle. Anyone original is suspect number one. (*Flicks through a magazine.*) Is this the latest issue?

WOMAN. Mmm. Hot off the press.

MAN. Who's she?

WOMAN. Her smile is so sunny. *Vogue*-amazing, no question. Megabucks. Mmm. Top model.

MAN (*points to another model*). And her?

WOMAN. *Vogue*-amazing, no question. Megabucks. Top model.

MAN. Top model? I like her.

WOMAN. How can you respect the IQ of a woman who earns her bucks strutting her stuff?

MAN. I think you'll find most guys aren't interested in her IQ.

WOMAN. I thought you were different.

MAN. I am different.

WOMAN. What makes you so different?

MAN. You tell me. (*Laughs. Reading from the magazine.*) 'Spring is here at last.' Listen to this. 'There's a new zing in the air. The rain-slicked streets are alive with friendly banter. You are a new woman who deserves her own space. For you unwittingly have said goodbye to fickle fate. You've had enough of other people's opinions. So what if the sun's shining or if the clouds are washed out. Perhaps you are like me, just sitting quietly on your own with a Martini or sipping a strong, dark cappuccino. Finally realising that the love of your life has lost its just-met tingle. And not knowing if you have the strength to push it away, or what kind of woman it takes to say finally 'it's over'. Love is many sided . . . ' I don't get it. Who invented this lingo? What's this guff about the weather? Is she trying to tell us how cool it is to sit in a café wearing shades, making a drama out of the 'dear John' for the toy boy, or is she just being a smarty-pants? Tell you what, I admire and despise these hacks. I really do. You've got to. Where do they get all that emotion, the endless uplift? The phoney bolster . . . You didn't write this, did you?

WOMAN. I'll tell you when you've finished reading it.

MAN. I've finished reading it. My back aches.

WOMAN. You stay in bed all day.

MAN. I didn't get much kip last night.

WOMAN. No?

MAN. Every time I was about to nod off, the phone rang. Four or five times it rang. So I shifted to the sofa. Got myself nice and comfy but this time it's not the phone. This time it's a bluebottle. Buzzz. Nearly daylight before the pester dwindles off. I put some music on and just lay there with the remote, flipping the same song over and over.

WOMAN. Are you going out later on?

MAN. Are you?

WOMAN. I'm just through the door . . . (*She sits and zaps the CD player into life.*) I wanted to ask you for a while now . . . you know more about it than me.

MAN. About what?

WOMAN. This. (*Pointing with the remote.*)

MAN. What about it?

WOMAN. The rhythm?

MAN. Here, give it me. (*He takes the remote and flips between the tracks.*) Listen. Listen to this bit. (*Drum and bass.*) That's rhythm. And this bit. (*Jazz.*) That's rhythm too. Hear it? This track's really tasty. The rhythm's a bit more complex. It's in there, hiding but not hiding. Ready to morph into something else. You can't hold onto it, can't imagine where it will slippery jig. It's like whisky. Fires you up. Like in a nightclub. You're burling round with your hand on her . . . Intimate and dangerous . . .You don't know what I'm talking about, do you? You only smile at cheap tunes. Boy bands. It's true.

WOMAN. There was never much rhythm with us, was there?

MAN (*suspiciously*). How do you mean? What made you say that?

WOMAN. What's the point talking? The same old ground. This has to end.

MAN. A bit o closure. Bring on the closure.

WOMAN. It has to.

MAN. When?

WOMAN. Soon.

MAN. I haven't found a flat yet.

WOMAN. You're here all the time. You never go out.

MAN. I'm not going to take any old dump.

WOMAN. I need to be on my own for a bit.

MAN. Is that what you needed when you moved in with him? You've shifted most of your stuff already. Clothes, CDs. Why are you being so measly about things? Is this the new you? More like how he wants you to be? What's happened? Letting other people boss you about. People you hardly know.

WOMAN. Being bossed about is better than being made a fool of.

MAN. I thought we weren't going to mention the past? I never pipped a squeak about what you were up to. So don't start.

WOMAN. You weren't interested. Did you care about me at all, ever?

MAN. Where's this coming from? If you're trying to get back at me, I understand. But know who is going to get clobbered the most? You. Mind that . . . By the way, we're going out tonight.

WOMAN. Pardon?

MAN. I forgot – Gran. We're going round for dinner. We better go. I said we would.

WOMAN. I'm tired.

MAN. Here, come on, let me rub your back. (*He rubs the back of her neck.*) See what you said about us – that rhythm stuff? How do you mean? What made you say that?

WOMAN. It's just like you to pull a fast one.

MAN. I'm trying to . . .

WOMAN (*pushing his hand away*). Any other services on offer? You know, there is only one difference between you and me, the obvious man/woman bit. Apart from that, looking at you is like looking at me in the mirror.

MAN. So when we were screwing, you were actually doing it with yourself. Think that's called masturbation.

WOMAN. More fun than doing it with you.

MAN. Do you think like that when you're with your new boy?

WOMAN. What's that to you?

MAN. I'm interested. In the truth.

WOMAN. I love him.

MAN. Surely not enough to marry the guy?

WOMAN. Yes. Strange as it may seem.

MAN. You've grown old. Totally carnaptious. (*Pause.*) Do you know Joey Yeung?

WOMAN. We did a feature on her ages ago.

MAN. I was out walking the other day, down by the canal. I got slightly lost. Went past this tiny metal shack, a shop selling music in fact, with metal windows and a metal door, crammed full of punters. It was sitting on its own on a piece of waste ground. Surrounded by high risers. As I got closer I could hear this singer singing, 'Why do you back-stab my sweet love?' I went in to ask who it was. Joey Yeung – singing her wee heart out. I stood there, listening to her tinsel voice. I was thinking if I ever met her I'd slip her a recipe for voice tonic. I actually bought one of her CDs, a special edition. You know me. When do I ever listen to that kind of trash? Canto pop.

WOMAN. There've always been excellent pop songs. You just don't pay attention, you never listen. I mean really listen. Not really.

MAN. Is that so? It's Thursday today. Give me a couple of days, Sunday, Monday at the most, and I'll have a place sorted.

They both sit not looking at each other, the sound of Formula One.

Scene Three

Early evening on Friday. WOMAN *and* WIFE *are in a rather run-down supermarket.* WIFE *is doing the shopping, pushing a trolley down one of the aisles. She is pregnant, not showing much.*

WIFE. Look at you. Your face looks terrible.

WOMAN. Really? It must be the lighting . . .

WIFE. Your hair.

WOMAN. What?

WIFE. It's a mess.

WOMAN. Who's going to be looking at me? My job doesn't depend on it.

WIFE. Bet things between you two are not as simple as you let on. I'm not daft. It's not the first time he's done it. Even I've seen him at it. Party flirt. Laughing . . . right there in front of me. You're sitting on a see-saw on your own, you are.

WOMAN. You should have let on – you never said.

WIFE. But you knew. What would be the point – me blabbing? So did you make a meal of it every time?

WOMAN. He won't change. That's what he's like.

WIFE. Why do you keep going back then? . . . I guess you should look on the bright side.

WOMAN. What bright side?

WIFE. The fact that he betrays you is a sign of respect. It is. Fancy-man has to have a plaything. You've got status where it counts, in his heart. If I was you, I'd want him to carry on playing around.

WOMAN. This time it's different. This time he's serious.

WIFE. Sure. The only thing different is the woman.

WOMAN. Don't laugh. He really cares about things. He does. He's got principles. He's clever and he's kind. He thinks he's not but he is. It's the way he watches things, the way he observes, that's what I mean about kind. I went back but I didn't expect to find him in. I just wanted to leave a note.

WIFE. Leave a note? That makes it so obvious you still love him. And that's your problem, his too, that you still worship him. But he's not worth it. He always has some kind of mysterious superiority complex. Please! Women should have a little self-respect. 'Nough said.

Pause.

I like this supermarket. I don't know why. It's always dead quiet. Like it's going out of business. Run-down shelves. Reminds me of how little I used to have.

What are you doing tonight?

WOMAN. I might go out. You?

WIFE. We got a new TV system. Over fifty channels. In five minutes I change channel six or seven times. So many chat shows. You don't know what's a spoof any more. You know where you are with the ads though. The sillier the better. What are you laughing at?

WOMAN. 'He always has some kind of mysterious superiority complex.'

WIFE. He does. Why do you always back him up to the hilt?

WOMAN. What's it like being married?

WIFE. Not much different from living together.

WOMAN. Why get married then?

WIFE. I started having boyfriends at eighteen. Fun, fun, fun, joke play-stuff, but if you're not married by twenty-nine, what are you doing? It was a big step for me to take. Really massive.

Hey, do you know any artists? You know, painters?

WOMAN. Yes, but they're all his chums.

WIFE. They're yours too. Our new house is too big, open plan. The walls feel so empty. They need some paintings. Oil paintings preferably. Abstracts are nice.

WOMAN. It's ok. I know your taste. I'll phone him. He knows a lot about painting.

WIFE. You should keep an eye on him. He's dangerous.

WOMAN. How so?

WIFE. Such high standards without the ability to reach them. It's simple.

WOMAN. No, you're wrong. He's a talented writer. I read his diary.

WIFE. That's naughty, don't tell me. There is no way, no way it's over between you two.

WOMAN. Yes it is.

WIFE. You read his diary?

WOMAN. My mind's made up, I'm getting wed and that's it. What do you think of him?

WIFE. Your IT Genius? If dot-com shares weren't going through the roof you wouldn't have slung him a second glance. He looks like a workaholic. He does.

WOMAN. Isn't your husband just the same?

WIFE. That's what men are supposed to do, bring the money home, earners. In my book that's the only yardstick men need to live up to. You can say I'm hard as pinballs but that's the way life's been for me.

WOMAN. He's a decent guy, your husband. Regular. Straight. How did he fall into your hands?

WIFE. Am I not regular too? Why does everyone say what a great bloke, really nice? I'm going to explode soon. I'm the one who's depressed here. With a belly like this. Why does everybody think it's such a great, smug, wonderful thing to be preggers?

WOMAN. You can hardly see it. You've always had a bit of a tummy. Voluptuous.

WIFE. That's what you think. What do you know?

WOMAN. Ok, I don't know. Calm down.

WIFE (*picks a pair of socks*). Do you like them? They are so cute. See the teeny bee motifs? Shall I buy them? I've already got a drawer full. Even I think that's out of order. But they're for my husband. How can you survive as a couple if you don't give each other little surprises? Every now and again. Do you like them? You're not into that kind of thing. Pressies. You're not like that.

WOMAN. I know.

WIFE. Fancy a coffee at Starbucks?

WOMAN. No.

WIFE. What about Baskin-Robbins? Thirty-one flavours.

WOMAN. When you get through all thirty-one flavours, know what comes along? Freaky flavour number thirty-two. I'm not in the mood.

WIFE. When I'm hungry I don't see properly. The world goes all wonky. Ok, I'll give you a lift over. IT's apartment block is near mine. The layout of his place is so crappy. Half the blueprint's not built yet.

WOMAN. No thanks – I prefer to take my life in my own hands.

WIFE. Are you on about my driving again – or dimple chin?

She holds her belly. The two women stand looking at each other for a few moments.

Scene Four

Friday evening – direct follow on from Scene Three. Outside the lift at YOUNGER BROTHER*'s apartment block. The lift numbers are going up. The light in the entrance is bright.*

WIFE. Oh, it's you. Is he back?

MAN. He's in. You know, I've never ever seen you empty-handed.

WIFE. Haven't you?

MAN. Big bags as usual. Posh nick-nacks, is it? (*Tries to look in her bags.*)

WIFE. Get off.

MAN. I'm not old fashioned, you know, about women not working but it is a bit thick you being so immune to earning, the way you spend it.

WIFE. What's the point being a career girl just to foot the bill for a man like you? Don't you get embarrassed? Using her money to entertain other women.

MAN. Oh, I always go Dutch. Every time. Even with her.

WIFE. That's even more sick.

MAN. I'm an even-handed guy.

WIFE. I've just left your ex-girlfriend.

MAN. How is she?

WIFE. She looks terrible. Like she hasn't looked in a mirror for days. Style sag and hair all over the place.

MAN. Style sag? No way. She could be going over a waterfall strapped to a log and she'd still be checking her smudge. Convinced her girlie-whirlie (*Mimes applying lipstick.*) will protect her from any . . . misfortune.

WIFE. How is your French student? What do you see in that hairy? What do you have to say to each other? I mean, has Mister Perfect turned into a total smut case? Pathetic.

MAN. I see you bought my brother yet more socks. How nice. Cheerio.

WIFE. Ciao.

Scene Five

Friday evening – direct follow on from Scene Four. On the sofa. The sound of a well-known soap opera on the TV. YOUNGER BROTHER *is appraising the shopping bags.*

WIFE *enters.*

WIFE. You forgot to put it down again.

YOUNGER BROTHER. What?

WIFE. The loo seat. There's more than one person in this house. What you waiting for? Turn it up.

YOUNGER BROTHER. You've seen this episode a million times.

WIFE. I want to see it again.

YOUNGER BROTHER (*producing a jar of coffee from one of the bags*). We never drink coffee.

WIFE. 'You should always buy something when you go somewhere.'

YOUNGER BROTHER (*mocking*). 'Or how else will you know you've been.' Yeah. (*Producing a whisk from another bag.*) Hey, I didn't know you could cook?

WIFE. I can't. It goes with the other stuff in there. That summer dumpling cookbook I bought. Else it won't look like a proper kitchen.

YOUNGER BROTHER (*producing socks*). How many pairs do you need?

WIFE. Most of them belong to you, darling.

YOUNGER BROTHER. I guess they do. Well, it could be

worse. At least you never bought any trainers, did you?

WIFE. Actually . . . (*She points to her feet.*)

YOUNGER BROTHER. Those aren't the old ones.

WIFE. I threw them away.

YOUNGER BROTHER. You binned them already? They weren't three weeks old.

WIFE. I need to feel good about myself. Brand new, just out the wrapper. Why can't you let me? You don't want me to be all miserable? I can't do it. I can't.

YOUNGER BROTHER (*holds her – pause*). I need to ask you . . . my brother, is it alright if he comes to stay with us – just a few days?

WIFE. No.

YOUNGER BROTHER. He can sleep in the spare room.

WIFE. No. We won't be able to make love. He should rent a place. Think about it.

YOUNGER BROTHER. Ok. I'll give him some funds.

WIFE. Our money? But there's loads of bills to pay this month. (*He pulls away.*) You said we had problems with cash flow.

YOUNGER BROTHER. Just forget it.

WIFE. Why can't you be happy?

YOUNGER BROTHER. I know you don't like him. Problem is he's my brother. I have to help him. I've only got the one older brother.

WIFE. I'm sorry, but it's not ok this time.

YOUNGER BROTHER. Fine. I'll call him tomorrow. I'm off to bed.

WIFE. Don't you want to chat?

YOUNGER BROTHER. I'm tired. Any idea how long I was stuck at my desk today? Any idea?

WIFE. I haven't eaten yet. I was waiting for you to call.

YOUNGER BROTHER. I don't want to eat.

WIFE. Too tired for munchies?

YOUNGER BROTHER. When do you get up compared to me? I leave in the morning and you're still asleep. What do you do all day?

WIFE. I picked up your suit from the dry cleaners.

YOUNGER BROTHER. Thanks.

WIFE. And all over with the hoover.

YOUNGER BROTHER. Thanks. Why don't we go to bed together?

WIFE. I won't be able to sleep now. Everybody around us is splitting up.

YOUNGER BROTHER. Is that what you want?

WIFE. I don't know. We don't have any major problems, do we? Away to bed. (*She sits holding her belly.*) We can talk about it in the morning.

YOUNGER BROTHER. Talk about what?

WIFE. You can see how big it is on the CT scan. Teeny.

YOUNGER BROTHER. Dimple chin?

WIFE. It's this long. (*She points her index finger and cocks her thumb like a pistol.*)

YOUNGER BROTHER. What did the doctor say?

WIFE. She said I should have it. It would be a shame to have an abortion now.

YOUNGER BROTHER. And what do you think?

WIFE. Me? I don't know what I think. I haven't made my mind up. The doctor said the longer you leave it, the more difficult the operation is.

YOUNGER BROTHER. Do you want to go through with it?

WIFE. Are you listening to a word I'm saying?

YOUNGER BROTHER. I am. I am.

WIFE. What about you? Do we want it or not?

YOUNGER BROTHER (*takes out a cigarette*). Don't get so het up. Things will sort themselves out.

WIFE. You're not allowed to smoke. Turn off the telly.

YOUNGER BROTHER (*turns off the TV*). Why is it you only want to talk when I'm ready for kip?

WIFE. I won't sleep now.

YOUNGER BROTHER. I've got to get up in the morning. What do you want me to do?

WIFE. Have you got any money on you?

YOUNGER BROTHER. In my jacket.

WIFE. I'm going out to eat.

YOUNGER BROTHER. There's spaghetti in the fridge.

WIFE. I don't fancy spaghetti. Alright?

YOUNGER BROTHER. Don't come back too late. (WIFE *exits.*) That's all I'm saying.

Scene Six

Saturday night – from here until the end of the play, all the action takes place on the same night. MAN *and* YOUNGER BROTHER *in a bar, playing pool. They have been drinking for a few hours now.*

MAN. Yours a double?

YOUNGER BROTHER. Ta. (*Lining up a shot.*)

MAN. How many's that now?

YOUNGER BROTHER. You or me? (*Takes the shot.*)

MAN. Me.

YOUNGER BROTHER. I don't know. Three? Four? I thought you just drank the vino?

MAN. Who the hell drinks wine while playing pool? Never seen that before: 'Languorously he sipped a cheeky Beaujolais before sinking the black.'

YOUNGER BROTHER. Don't start with the lectures. (*Takes another shot.*)

MAN. Today doesn't feel like a red-wine day – Ok?

YOUNGER BROTHER. You upset about something?

MAN. Not at all. I nearly always feel my head is . . . empty.

YOUNGER BROTHER. Here. Listen to this one. (*Lines up shot.*)

MAN. What?

YOUNGER BROTHER. How many days in this month?

MAN. Thirty-one.

YOUNGER BROTHER. Check again. Know how many days I've been rostered for this month at the office? Thirty-nine. (*Sinks the ball.*)

MAN. That's not right.

YOUNGER BROTHER. Double-booked by Personal Development and Planning. You can't tell anybody. Upstairs won't listen. They say what you said, 'It's not right.'

MAN. You're a busy man, right enough.

YOUNGER BROTHER. What do you think? What does it mean?

MAN. It's what the system is – pure whimsy. If I was you I wouldn't bother about it.

YOUNGER BROTHER. Too right. There's not much I can do about it. (*Lines up another shot.*) I was round at FESCO this morning registering for Business English. I'm up to

here. Got to do Accountancy for the final unit of my MBA
next month. (*Misses.*)

MAN. I thought you were going for your law licence. (*Lines
up shot.*)

YOUNGER BROTHER. I am. I'm always thinking about more
qualifications. I'm always thinking there's one more
diploma I could do with. There's two new interns at work,
couple of clipes. In meetings they stare at me like tigers
eyeing up lunch. I can feel the hairs bristle on my ticker.
How is it pimply geeks grow up so fast? Do you think I've
got what it takes . . . to be a top-flight manager?

MAN. How difficult is it to be a fuckin good manager? Pretend
like everyone else. (*Lines up shot.*) You're not stupid, you
know the score. Invest in an Armani suit and instead of
going out for lunch eat al desko. If you get into a (*Takes
shot and misses.*) position of power, screw up big time, that
way you're guaranteed more promotion. It's one of the laws
of business.

YOUNGER BROTHER. You don't have a clue. (*He lines up a
shot.*) You look for a new job for me. It won't be easy. The
climate's not right. Besides, if I can't hack this number,
what job can I do? There's no point taking unnecessary
risks. (*Sinks a ball. He laughs.*)

MAN. What have you got to laugh about?

YOUNGER BROTHER. What you said to that bar girl. Earlier
on.

MAN. What?

YOUNGER BROTHER. You said folk who don't work
actually enjoy their weekends a lot more than grafters.

MAN. It's obvious to me.

YOUNGER BROTHER. Not to her it wasn't, or me.

MAN. At weekends the street's full of cyclists, right? But by
the time I get up during the week the rush hour is long
gone. I miss seeing that – bikes crowding down the street.
I miss the briskness. The energy of those little machines,

spokes whirling. And the faces. Each one a bit wild, gasping after some weird dream that they . . . they are the most important. They don't see how odd they look, how odd the world looks. They actually think their day has come.

YOUNGER BROTHER. People work too hard to think like that. Everybody's under the cosh, there's constraints in everybody's life, restrictions, especially folk on bikes.

MAN. That the slick mob in motors talking?

YOUNGER BROTHER. What? You think there's something up with me having a motor? I need it to shoot about in. Clients expect it. One day everyone will have one. No more bikes. You too. It's a 'clear trend'.

MAN. And to acquire the spanking brand-new motor what do you have to do? Commute to a tower block full of cubicles. Sit there all day talking into a telephone thinking of pay day. Courses in politeness. How to wear the company smile when you're giving some chump the brush off. You're only a number man. Replaceable. Is that the kind of life people really want? See me, I choose not to.

YOUNGER BROTHER. Wow, old comrade, take it easy. (*Lines up shot.*) When people are in their twenties they're skint, irate, angry – right? – and that's the way it should be. But if you're like that in your thirties – boy, you're in soapy bubble. What's happened? It's only two days since I last saw you. How come, all of a sudden, you've turned into a total dimwit? (*Sinks the black.*) I win.

MAN. Good game. I'm a bit rusty.

YOUNGER BROTHER. I've noticed – your hands. They shake. You should check yourself, go easy on the spirits.

MAN. Helps get me to sleep. I know it's not a good idea. I don't plan to become an alkie.

YOUNGER BROTHER. You're half-cut already. But you're not too bad. When you're really drunk you start speaking English. Top-shit twaddle, old boy. One more game?

MAN. Set them up.

YOUNGER BROTHER (*salutes* MAN *with his drink*). 'China Can Say No!' – but you aren't able to . . . I'll set them up. What's the matter?

MAN. Do you remember? That's what our French friend used to say.

YOUNGER BROTHER. Yeah. It was his number one drinking slogan. 'China Can Say No – but we aren't able to!' His accent was gob-awful, tones all over the job.

MAN. The girl at the bar said he died.

YOUNGER BROTHER. No way.

MAN. He went back home. Nearly ten years here he was. Found Paris wasn't what he expected. Completely bored. Ended up in Brazil. São Paulo. That's where he got done in. In a bar. Shot. That's what she said.

YOUNGER BROTHER. Maybe he was playing his guitar at the time. He was crap.

MAN. Yeah, and once he started, eh?

YOUNGER BROTHER. His busking used to empty the street. (*Pause.*) Dead? Shit. How old was he?

MAN. Thirty-three. Jesus died when he was thirty-three.

YOUNGER BROTHER. I don't get it. What's Jesus got to do with anything?

MAN. Not a bad way to leave the stage. Bang! Nice and simple. Gets rid of a lot of hassle. Skips that Buddhist thing about bad news being hard to dodge.

YOUNGER BROTHER. If he'd stayed in China he'd still be alive.

MAN. What was his name? What did we call him again?

YOUNGER BROTHER. I've totally forgotten. (*Snaps his fingers.*) Dessailly!

MAN. Dessailly? He's the captain of the '98 French football team.

YOUNGER BROTHER (*pause*). Jacquet!

MAN. That's the manager's name, clot.

YOUNGER BROTHER. So it is.

MAN. This is going to bug me.

YOUNGER BROTHER. My memory's bust. I'll look through my name cards when I get home.

MAN. Yakai? We did actually call him . . . Jacquet.

YOUNGER BROTHER. That's what I meant – Yakai! I knew . . .

MAN. But that's not him.

YOUNGER BROTHER. What do you mean, it's not him?

MAN. Of course it's not him. It's what we called him. Just like at work you're called Daniel. But who's Daniel? Are you Daniel? It's a fake handle. It doesn't mean anything.

YOUNGER BROTHER. But that is me – I am DANIEL! (*He's wearing an ID tag.*)

MAN. You don't get it.

YOUNGER BROTHER. What don't I get? Are we talking about Daniel or Yakai?

MAN. His name is not Yakai. Forget Yakai. He never existed.

YOUNGER BROTHER. But you just said, the bar girl said, he croaked it.

MAN. The person who died wasn't YAKAI!

YOUNGER BROTHER. You're being pedantic.

MAN. What's the point? When we were kids, *Tom and Jerry* was way over your head.

YOUNGER BROTHER. What you trying to say? That I'm shallow – some sort of infant?

MAN. Listen. Little brother. The word Yakai doesn't MEAN anything. The name and him have nothing to do with each other.

YOUNGER BROTHER. You think too much about stuff, man.

MAN. I'm trying to understand who he really was. There's a person behind our little joke label.

YOUNGER BROTHER. Naw – you just feel guilty. Guilty because you bedded his girlfriend.

MAN. Don't go there.

YOUNGER BROTHER. You've discovered your conscience? Well done, Yakai. Come on, let's drink, a toast in honour of the poor sod's life.

MAN. In honour of his life? I'm going to the Gents.

YOUNGER BROTHER. Drink your drink first. Then you and your toast can go to the loo together.

Scene Seven

In a different bar. WIFE *is sitting on a sofa.* WOMAN *enters, she's wearing a miniskirt, she's so tipsy, she has to hold on to things.*

WIFE. Look at you. You're staggering in figures of eight. Margaritas are so nice.

WOMAN. What shall I have now? (*Picks up the cocktail menu.*) A Mummy, a Sex on the Beach, a KGB, or a Snogger's Delight?

WIFE. A Mummy is non-alcoholic. I'm driving.

WOMAN. You left your car at home.

WIFE. So I did. Let's have an orange juice anyway. Smokers need extra vitamin C.

WOMAN. Where did you learn that?

WIFE. From your magazine. Don't you read it? I've got one in my bag. There's a bit on how Demi Moore uses mineral water to bath in. And how Madonna squanders a million a year on PR. Every time I read it, it does my head in. Where do you find these *Vogue*-amazings, mmm? I bet they don't smoke, or binge drink, just pure spring water. Look. (*Holds magazine up.*) Look. When did you ever see teeth that white? It's the only reason they laugh, ha ha ha, so they can put their teeth on display. At the end of the night they don't have to . . .

TOGETHER. . . . linger hopefully . . .

WIFE. . . . for last dances. A total stranger with plenty money is always waiting on them. Look at us.

WOMAN. I have quit running after men.

WIFE. Oh? Then why are you wearing that skirt?

WOMAN. What's wrong with trying to look sexy once in a while?

WIFE. You look like some old guy's favourite tart.

WOMAN. Why are you always putting me down?

WIFE. Sorry – but you are two-faced. You are. IT Genius hasn't seen you in that skirt, has he?

WOMAN. Cigarette?

WIFE. Ta. This song reminds me of old times – even though it's not like it's ages ago or anything. You know, when I see my old boyfriends they say I've matured. They don't tell us we're growing old, do they? They say 'you've ripened'. Flanelling women our age. Don't you think it's scary the amount of men you've slept with?

WOMAN. I'm not you.

WIFE. You don't exactly hold on tight. Even before you found IT Genius you had a couple of men on the go.

WOMAN. How do you know?

WIFE. I've decided it's time I was interested in other people's lives. Not just my own.

WOMAN. 'Why hang yourself from the one tree when there are so many to choose from?'

WIFE. That's a gory one. You're quoting your ex, I bet. You've started mimicking him, talking heavy-duty, death and life shit. Like suddenly you're a philosopher or something.

WOMAN. History, that's what he studied at uni.

WIFE. Oh, the gifted scholar. The man's a sham. What talent?

WOMAN. I've never ever heard him say a bad word about you. All the time we lived together. Why don't you like him? You can tell me, it's ok, it's over between us.

WIFE. When we got married, he was there at the do after. He says to one of his cronies, while I'm topping them up, as if I wasn't there, 'Being married is a bit of a bum deal.' Another time after, when I brought a group of friends home and he was there and he butts in: 'I could tell you were from Shanxi province the moment you opened your mouth. Only people from Shanxi province call a room a house.'

WOMAN. He wasn't trying to be rude.

WIFE. Yes he was. I can't stand the mocking smile on his face.

WOMAN. You're imitating him now.

They both imitate his smile.

WIFE. You know his scoff face. But I tell you the thing that really got me. After the wedding when they all crowded into the bridal suite to see us on our way so to speak, he was there again with my husband's workmates. His boss, the lot. You know the tease where the guy stands on a chair with an apple and asks the bride and groom to take a bite, then at the last moment pulls it away so our mouths meet and kiss? Well, we've done it a couple of times and everybody's cheering, then he pipes up: 'I've never seen such a shameless bride.' I wanted everybody to leave after that. What were his parents thinking I was like. I'm screaming 'leave' and everyone's laughing drunk, throwing apples onto the bed. I know it was a joke but he really hurt me like a punch. You can't stand that about him either, can you? His so-called 'sense of humour'.

WOMAN. You're too touchy. Me and him are better off as friends.

WIFE. How come everybody says that after they break up?

WOMAN. You don't understand the way it was between us.

WIFE. Was shagging all and sundry just one of his many fine attributes?

WOMAN. Nobody knows what makes a relationship tick. But it's true, breaking up is a relief – for both of us. We should have done it a long time ago. We dragged it out for too long.

WIFE. But you only met IT recently.

WOMAN. It has even less to do with him. He's just the fuse.

WIFE. If it wasn't for IT, you two would still be sitting there, sipping tea together, kidding on there wasn't a bad taste in your mouths.

WOMAN. I tholed – that's my granny's word. I tholed so much, not cos I'm feeble or scared, cos I'm not, or because I'm begging to be loved, but just not to have regrets. That's the worst thing. What I can't stand. That I might have regrets. That's why I stuck it.

WIFE. He's the one who'll live to regret it. He's the one who's hurting now.

WOMAN. His face is expressionless.

WIFE. What people feel isn't always written on their faces. Men are different from us. They can't express themselves. And then when finally they do, they explode. If men broke down easily there would be no hope in the world. None. There would be no MasterCard or world's tallest building. (*They laugh.*) But you seem alright now. In the past, I remember, when I chucked someone I used to cry myself into a right mess. I think I'm strange.

WOMAN. Yeah. Should I cry? I can't seem to.

WIFE. You don't try to make men like you that much, do you? But you knew how to be cute with him. All girlie-whirlie.

WOMAN. With who, which one?

WIFE. Him, your ex, of course. 'Which one?' Don't you remember the first time you met him? He was sitting there, where you're sitting. And you were here. You were tipsy girl, and your face was all red. In the mood for love. You couldn't stop talking about that film director you both admired.

WOMAN. Wong Kar Wai.

WIFE. Questions back and forth. Don't you think your enthusiasm for Wong Kar Wai went a bit too far? How about you and IT? Does he have much talk – anything to say for himself?

Pause.

WOMAN. We treat each other with the respect accorded to guests. That's all I want now out of life.

WIFE (*snorts*). I give up. You do my head in. If that's the life you want, go ahead and marry him.

WOMAN. At the end of the day, he lost me. He won't find another able to endure what I had to, for so long. It was my choice. Now he sees that student with the 36 double-D tits. Thinks of herself as alternative and carefree when she's actually boring and manky inside.

WIFE. She's from Anhui province. What do you expect?

WOMAN. Works as a part-time nanny. She can speak French but her own tongue's rubbish. And French is never ever pleasant to listen to either, is it? The whole world likes speaking English. Why? Because only English has rhythm.

WIFE. Here we go again.

WOMAN. What do you think . . .

WIFE. . . . rhythm is? So like a dumped woman scratching the same bit. Women don't just attract men on the strength of their conversational style, other ingredients are involved. Look at the way you're smoking, rapid lung sucks. Not elegant like so. It's cos you lack love.

The two women stare into space for a while.

WOMAN. Do I really look that bad? Three years, one mistake and he dumps me without the merest dog fart of a hint.

WIFE. I know what you're going through. Like all of us, you want him to still care even though it's over. But you finished it. You found a new man. That's cool. Life is for living. I fancy a dance.

WOMAN. What about your husband? Call him and see if he wants to come over.

WIFE. He's doing overtime. He's too busy.

WOMAN. He won't want to hang out with us anyway. (*She touches her face.*) My jaded face and you too plump for fascinating.

WIFE. Do we look old? Let's go dance.

Exit.

Scene Eight

The men are already in the bar. They enter, carrying bottles of beer.

MAN. Check the bum and thighs on her.

YOUNGER BROTHER. Where?

MAN. There, floating right there in front of us. All soft and springy.

YOUNGER BROTHER. Majestic legs.

MAN. Like a racehorse prancing round the paddock. (*He sighs.*) There are more and more sexy babes about. Trouble is, they don't look my way, not any more. Outrageous, eh?

YOUNGER BROTHER. You've had your share. The full unexpurgated peeve, man. I haven't been with anybody since I got wed.

MAN. Not once? You're kidding.

YOUNGER BROTHER. No jest. Sometimes, I get a charge. Well, in my heart things go a bit loopy. To say the least. But the wife spots it right away.

MAN. I don't believe it.

YOUNGER BROTHER. She'll say, 'Hey darling, you seem a bit troubled at the moment, you're all fidgety. Ants in your pants.' So I blank it. In the end they're all the same. This afternoon I went with the PR department to see some clients. All eight of our PR people are women. You should hear them. Yak yak. Boyfriends, husbands, style quiff, shops, how to spend their wed-sucker's dosh. Ten minutes of that and I'm numb all over.

MAN. Boring.

YOUNGER BROTHER. One woman's plenty. You should see mine shop. Never looks back over her shoulder. That's why I don't ask her to work – she'd just tan the lot in the shops.

MAN. Your wife's quality. She's far more intelligent than you.

YOUNGER BROTHER. And what about your ex-girlfriend?

MAN. She's ok.

YOUNGER BROTHER. And the new lumber?

MAN. What do you think?

YOUNGER BROTHER. Appearances can be deceptive. I think she's not as dolly dimple as she looks.

MAN. At last! We concur. Well, there's a first time for everything.

YOUNGER BROTHER. Piss off! Know what my wife says about you? She says, 'Your brother thinks screwing around is some sort of tonic for female depression.'

MAN (*sighs*). The other night I was watching the motor racing. I must have dozed cos suddenly it's me going round and round. One minute I'm driving, the next I'm running. Running in a relay race. I haven't a clue why. Then everybody's sitting up in the stands and I'm the only guy out there still legging it but the baton's vanished. I kept running up to different women, each one wants to improve me. But I couldn't bring myself to say, 'Yes, ok, I'll hand over my whole life to you.' I kept answering, 'I insist on perfection, I know I do, but I won't hope for love. I don't believe in it.' I kept saying that. Why am I telling you this?

YOUNGER BROTHER. You're a bit old for gibbering baloney. But don't fret, you've held on to your looks. You can still reel in the girls and laugh in the face of danger. (*They laugh.*) How's the work going? You've been writing for a year now.

MAN. More or less.

YOUNGER BROTHER. You should do a martial-arts novel, a blockbuster. Make some serious money.

MAN. We're miles apart, you and me. Only, I can write what I need to write about. Perhaps you think I'm full of myself?

YOUNGER BROTHER. I was going to ask you to recommend a good read but I think I'll pass. You still working on the same novel?

MAN. No, it's new. It's about love and death – a guy sort of in heavy regret for his own life.

YOUNGER BROTHER. So it's a comedy, right?

MAN. You're not interested – hey, that's ok. I don't expect you to be.

YOUNGER BROTHER. I won't ask, then. I bet I won't be able to understand it anyway.

MAN. 'All men kill the thing they love. The coward does it with a kiss. The brave man with a sword.'

YOUNGER BROTHER. Ah, a yarn about a sword-swallower.

MAN. I can't discuss serious stuff with you. It's a quote.

YOUNGER BROTHER. I know it's a quote. You think I don't?

MAN. Want to hazard a guess where from? For entertainment's sake.

YOUNGER BROTHER. Why do you always look down your nose at me? It's Oscar Wilde. (*He takes a deep breath.*) 'Oscar Wilde was a representative of the aesthetic school of literature. He was popular for a short time during the 1890s for his eccentric and peculiar dress and behaviour as well as his shocking views on literature. After leaving university for London he became a celebrity in society circles. His aphoristic style is adept. In today's terms the two reasons he became famous are no longer desirable. One: it is not possible to perfect his theory of literature as in this world there are no persons who can practise art just for art's sake. And two: his lifestyle brought about his downfall and hard labour on the treadmill.'

MAN. What a surprise – you do know something after all.

YOUNGER BROTHER. You forget. When I was swotting to get into arts school I used to memorise all kinds of rubbish. Out-of-date encyclopedias, periodicals, whatever. It was easy – like eating chocolate. Brain like a sponge. I haven't forgotten a thing.

MAN. The way I remember, you didn't get past the entrance exam?

YOUNGER BROTHER. You were away at Gran's for the summer. Dad had other ideas. He never let me take the exam. My marks were top notch. I even got one of my paintings exhibited. But still, he wasn't convinced I could make it as a painter. He'd say the competition's too stiff. And if I didn't get in, then my other studies would suffer. And how would I catch up? He told me it was safer to keep painting as a 'wee sideline'.

MAN. He never let you sit the exam? You never were any good at sticking up for yourself. Convictions are for other people, eh?

YOUNGER BROTHER. It was Dad's call. His decision. I know after, when I told him the sort of talent that made it, the plodders that kept trying, he felt he'd let me down. You know the old man? Kept his mouth zipped but you could always tell what he was feeling. I woke up one night, ages

later and he's standing there in the dark at the bottom of my
bed. He says to me, 'Do you still want to sit the exam?'
I says, 'No. What's the point?' I hadn't practised. 'I'm too
far behind everybody else.' He thought I might have regrets.
He thought I might hate him. I felt shit for a while. If you'd
been home I might have went down another road. You knew
how to fight them. All my colour studies are still in a
cardboard box on the balcony. I should have tried. When I
go and see an exhibition I wonder, if I was still painting
would I be as good as the stuff on the walls? I'll never
know. I should have tried, stretched myself then made a
decision. Best not to dwell on it. Dad pushed me down the
wrong road.

MAN. It's your own fault – you can't dump the blame on
someone else.

YOUNGER BROTHER. It's his fault too, right? He could have
encouraged me?

MAN. Dad's old school. All his life he's had to watch it. Every
step taken a prudent tiptoe. But you could have brought him
round. The key thing is you don't believe in yourself. You
still fudge it. Like your wife's up the duff and you're
running round asking work colleagues if yous should have
the baby. You asked the canteen lady her opinion yet? It's
not up to them. It's up to you to figure out if yous want it or
not.

YOUNGER BROTHER. I don't want it.

MAN. There you go.

YOUNGER BROTHER. But it's a life, eh?

MAN. So have it. It will give Mum and Dad something to do.
Look how they pamper the cat. Like a little Emperor. They
can't rely on me to produce the wonder kid.

YOUNGER BROTHER. Yeah, but my wife's adamant she's
against it. In the end it's up to her. It's her body not mine.
She's got the final say. It would save a lot of hassle if we
didn't go for it. Give me a bit of space for a wee while yet.

MAN. And in a couple of years' time she'll still say no.

YOUNGER BROTHER. In a couple of years, worries about the old body-clock will kick in.

MAN. Ever the optimist. Can I ask – are you like this at work? Maybe aye, maybe no.

YOUNGER BROTHER. I'm not the boss. Upstairs don't like staff with motor mouths.

MAN. Your mouth stays zipped cos it's not in you to make a decision.

YOUNGER BROTHER. Is criticising folk a long-term project of yours?

MAN. You're not pleased with what I just said? Can you give me an example, however small, of a decision you've actually made on your own?

YOUNGER BROTHER. Why are you always lecturing me?

MAN. It's way too late to give you any lectures. You'll never learn. See, some people just need other people to tell them what to do.

YOUNGER BROTHER. I admit I don't have the same determination as you. Granny brought you up, and Mum and Dad never once hindered you. You pleased yourself. Just my luck to be born last.

MAN. You're putting yourself down again – Junior.

YOUNGER BROTHER. You forget plenty. At home you acted like Mum and Dad's equal. You did. When I came in, it was nag nag nag. Half an hour hammering away at some minor fault on my part. Not polite, the way they knocked on your bedroom door. If I forgot to turn the loo light off, it was an act of utter and total selfishness. Disregard on a world-shattering scale. I'm married, I've got a career and they still favour you. I don't get it. I just don't get it.

MAN. If it's any consolation, neither do I.

YOUNGER BROTHER. There's something wrong with the way we were brought up.

MAN. I hope I was ok. Not the world's worst older brother.
What do you recall? Any good points?

YOUNGER BROTHER. You wore good gear. Nice shoes. Old-
style Converse.

MAN. I've got them on. (*Pulls up his trousers.*) Dad brought
them back from a trip abroad. I found them in my room
under the bed when I was packing. Still a snug fit. My feet
haven't grown in seventeen years. I look down and wonder
if they belong to me. Was it me that really wore them? Were
my feet always that far away? It's bonkers.

YOUNGER BROTHER. What's bonkers?

MAN. I always feel my head is thirty-three and my feet are
still in secondary school.

YOUNGER BROTHER. What's that? Soya sauce?

MAN. Blood. I was in a rush, late for basketball training when
I tangled with a cyclist. It's his. My team handle was Big
Foot. Number-one shirt. I really miss that – jump and slam
dunk! Hanging there in a sky hook. The deck . . . gone. The
ground wiped out. During training days the girls from
fourth year would come over, stand in the shadows
watching us. Some truly well-developed beauties.

YOUNGER BROTHER. You think they were clocking you?

MAN. If I knew then what I know now. What's the point in
looking back at all this?

YOUNGER BROTHER. I think we need another drink.

MAN. Let's shift somewhere else. She comes here – I don't
want to bump into her.

YOUNGER BROTHER. What are you scared of? Scared she'll
say something?

MAN. I'm scared of the letdown. I'm talking about myself.
Betrayal, separation, then together again. And all over
again: betrayal, split-up and then together again. Why do
people keep repeating the same mistakes?

YOUNGER BROTHER. Do you love her?

MAN. If she walked in just now, I don't know what I'd feel. Where shall we go?

YOUNGER BROTHER. Up to you.

MAN. Where do you usually go?

YOUNGER BROTHER. Anywhere is cool.

MAN. Well, where do you fancy?

YOUNGER BROTHER. I don't usually hang out this late.

MAN. Are you tired?

YOUNGER BROTHER. No.

MAN. You can shoot off home if you want to.

YOUNGER BROTHER. It's ok. I'll hang around. Keep you company for a bit.

MAN. Shall we toss a coin to see where we're going – let it decide? Look at the state of this joint. Done up like an old teahouse. It used to be an old teahouse, for real. Check the polystyrene beams. The half-arsed fakes. But has anything really changed? People still yacking – ok, it's modern guff, but have we really moved on? A theme bar whose antique pokes through – how funny is that?

They exit.

Scene Nine

In the bar. The women re-enter. WIFE has been sick in the Ladies and WOMAN is supporting her, carrying her shoes.

WOMAN. You're pinching my arm.

WIFE. I can breathe – fresh air.

WOMAN. You missed the sinks – by a mile . . .

WIFE. I feel awful.

WOMAN. . . . You threw up all over her frock. Nobody would guess you're pregnant, would they? Come on – I'm taking you home.

WIFE. Let me sit for a bit, please. Shit . . . tomorrow I've got a hospital appointment.

WOMAN. How far gone is it?

WIFE. Three months. At first I thought I had a virus. My period's never regular anyway. This pregnancy is an illness, I'm telling you.

WOMAN. I'd keep it if I was you. Unplanned kids are often clever.

WIFE (*sighs*). You know what they say . . . about the clever kid? It carries a 'fragile lantern'. Let it be average, please.

WOMAN. There's a thought.

WIFE. I still don't get if there's any point at all to my life. How can I bring into the world another fuddled little mite?

WOMAN. It will all make sense once you have it.

WIFE. You think so? My sister says so. She was always dead ambitious but she's just too ordinary. Her husband's worse. He's gullible and weak. They're going nowhere fast. Everything they want is so out of reach. Now her kid is her future. The family's only hope. Their poor kid. Imagine putting that on a kid. He looks like a piece of rind. I've always liked little tots. I have. I go all weepy when I'm washing or something and you see: 'Please keep this product out of reach of children.' Kids are so adorable.

WOMAN. What did you study at uni? Your logic is beyond me.

WIFE. I told you before.

WOMAN. Something 'Mickey Mouse'.

WIFE. HIN-DI as in Hindi.

WOMAN. Doesn't everybody speak English in India?

WIFE. Exactly. Not much point in knowing Hindi. Studying something so useless was the only way to get here. Likewise to get my residency after graduation I applied to a uni work unit, specialising in – guess what?

WOMAN. Hindi.

WIFE. The department was on its last legs. Each morning I'd stuff my crappy bag full of crappy Hindi books and go to work on the underground. I spent months listening to brainwashed old professors trying to teach me translation. Old parchment fingers trying to preserve Hindi vocab, Hindi grammar for ever. Why? Please, after a while my brain was screaming, 'No more Hindi.' I'm Chinese. Luckily the place was shut down and I got the stamp: 'Laid-off worker.' So then cos I'm long-term unemployed I got a permanent residency, which is an even bigger joke than having to study Hindi to stop here.

WOMAN. Poor thing. Some people are too full of previous experience. No wonder you've decided to let your husband provide for you.

WIFE. Nothing up with that. He wants to provide for me – he's totally cool about it. You could say he's helping the government out.

Both laugh.

WOMAN. Yes – what he's taken on is a national responsibility.

WIFE. What do you want me to do? Be like the wives in our block, drive a luxury BMW and do a pretend job with a pretend salary? You couldn't run a moped on what they earn. It's all fake so they can swan about like they're so high class, so personally successful, with such great families and great jobs. They just want to fool the rest of us.

WOMAN. Do you think I fall into that 'pretend' category?

Pause.

WIFE. It's not for me to say. You are unlucky. You are a woman with a bitter destiny. Get your fortune read, it's what I'd do if I was you.

WOMAN. And find out what? That I don't have a life outside
my job, just so that I can feel good about my career at
college reunions? I know what I'm like. I don't need to go
to a fortune teller. I can work it out for myself.

WIFE. You didn't work it out with him.

WOMAN. What happened, happened. I went down a certain
road knowing how it would turn out. A bitter pill of my own
choosing. I deserve the mess I'm in. What I don't want is
anybody's sympathy.

WIFE. Come on. You decided ages ago you couldn't see a
future with him.

WOMAN. So? I hung around waiting for him to find what he
really wanted – before saying 'it's over'. I don't want him
to be unhappy.

WIFE. That was really nice of you! But he never read your
diary. I had a boyfriend did that to me. I was raging. How
dare he? Like he scrubbed a window mist peering in at my
private stuff, leaving me no distance at all. So I burned it. I
didn't write any more. That was a blunder. Now I would be
able to read about all the nutty larks I got up to. Nothing
heavy. Nothing nobody else hasn't done or pretended. But if
my hubby read it? It would be evidence for the prosecution.
I was right to burn them. People need their mystery –
especially us. I only ever had one favour to ask the guys I
went with – don't get me pregnant, please. They all
managed not to.

WOMAN. This is your first time then?

WIFE. Of course it is. In that regard at least I remain faultless.
No babies or abortions. But I tell you, I'm scared. Scared of
it. This tiny grub thing inside you grows bigger every day.
Always stuffing your face. Scran you wouldn't normally
scoff. And puking. Yuk. The first time I went to the hospital
I saw this young just-out-the-wrapper locum. If he wasn't a
bad doctor, then he was definitely a virgin. He told me I had
irritable bowel syndrome. Wrote me a prescription for a
whole cabinet of foreign pills and lotions – idiot!

WOMAN. It's best not to know. A fool has a fool's luck. I'm glad you've never gone through a termination. The pain is different. The second time, I was in hospital cos of him. In Guangzhou. I remember it was summer and the whole city stank of overripe durian fruit. There were three girls waiting in the ward with me. They looked like their faces had been dusted with flour. Pale with fear they were. Nobody was with them. The first one rested just twenty minutes. She said she had only taken an hour off work and had to go cos it was a trip by bicycle. My ex tried to foist on her something for the taxi – 'It's faster by taxi,' he said, 'much faster,' but she just kept saying no and then crying. When I was lying on the rubber, the doctor ticked off questions. 'Are you wed?' 'I am,' I lied. 'Is this your first pregnancy?' 'Yes,' I lied. There was a geranium on the window sill. A dusty old thing. I just turned my head and focused on it and all the time I was thinking: 'Why such a high price for wanting so little happiness?' I bit my lip. I would not cry, like the girl from the factory. (*Pause.*) Well, I deserved it – didn't I?

WIFE. You have to take precautions.

WOMAN. Don't do what I did. That's all I'm saying. I know you're thinking of Guangzhou. Keep it. Don't commit murder. Think of the baby, poor unborn thing, it has a soul too.

WIFE. I know. I think about it all the time – just vanishing without having seen what Mummy and Daddy look like.

WOMAN. I've committed some real sins. I know what I'm talking about . . . What are you whispering?

WIFE. Hindi. It's a blessing for your children's souls. Asking them to forgive you. Rama is the top Hindu deity.

WOMAN. Thanks. I don't think they will forgive me.

WIFE. You didn't plan it. You're not a bad person.

WOMAN. Will they know what you're saying? I mean, they never spoke Hindi.

WIFE. We're talking religion here – course they'll know.

WOMAN. Can we please go now?

WIFE. Let's. It's not the place for dimple chin, is it? The ambience is a bit mental.

WOMAN. Your feet should be up on the sofa. Listening to bubble music. Get him to pamper you.

WIFE. Give me a second. The Ladies calls – again.

WOMAN. Don't be long.

> WIFE *exits.* WOMAN *picks up a newspaper lying on the table. Reads.* WIFE *returns.*

WIFE. Guess who I just saw?

WOMAN. Who?

WIFE. Someone you're dying to bump into.

WOMAN. He's here?

WIFE. No! That French-speaking nanny from Anhui. The student he's seeing. She's with an ugly foreigner – red hair – a real horse's head. Happy now?

WOMAN. I don't care about her. Look, have you seen this?

Hands her the paper. WIFE *looks at it briefly before handing it back.*

WIFE. I've not got my contacts in. What's it about?

WOMAN. It's about the cost of babies. From little to adolescent. The list is endless. Couples are put off by the cost. It says education, health care and clothing are all substantial expenses.

In the original production the actress selected only a few statistics from the original article below. Some of the figures are incorrect as in the original.

Education costs: 13 years of overseas schooling on average 10,000 US\$ per year. 13 years of Chinese schooling on average 27,000 People's Currency per year.

Health costs: Consultations – 35 to 85 US\$ per visit.

Orthodontic treatment: 50 US$ per visit.

Dental care: 20 US$ per visit.

Sight correction: 95 US$ per visit.

Immunisation: 20 to 75 US$.

Overnight hospital stays: Approximately 100 US$ a night. For one child, with one visit to the doctor per year at 50 US$, and one immunisation, at 50 US$ the total for 13 years will be 3,445 US$.

Board: Based on figures for a three-bedroom apartment or villa, including water, electricity, cooking gas and central heating. 1 year costs 24,000 People's Currency or 3,000 US$. So, 13 years will be 20,800 People's Currency. 26,000 US$.

Food: Based on figures for three meals a day of principally Western or Chinese food. If you have a child these costs will increase. On average, in one month you will pay 2000 People's Currency, which makes a total of 240,000 People's Currency a year, that's 30,000 US$. For 13 years that makes 312,000 People's Currency or 40,000 US$.

Clothes: On average 50 US$ a month which makes 600 US$ per year, and 7,800 for 13 years. The above figures represent a rough calculation and will not be the same for every family unit.

WIFE. Why are you showing me this evil thing? (*Ripping up the newspaper.*) Just as I decide to put down the executioner's knife you show me all this?

WOMAN. What are you doing?

WIFE. I'm scared. (*She stuffs the torn paper into her bag.*) This way I won't have to look at it again. You have no idea. You don't understand the pain of a materialist. No thanks. No thanks.

WIFE *exits.* WOMAN *is alone.*

Scene Ten

The two men are walking through the city. Night.

MAN. Has it gone twelve yet?

YOUNGER BROTHER. Just after one actually. Where next then?

MAN. Not many places open this time and the ones that are, are full of coke-heads. Scoffing their medicine. Bores, eh? Even when they're flying they're dullards.

YOUNGER BROTHER. What about that new place? It's just opened?

MAN. It will be full of web wannabes, talking about their Flash, their Poser skills. 'How much RAM have you got?'

YOUNGER BROTHER. Networking?

MAN. TALKing about art. You can't tell if they're idle shites or waiting for inspiration. Don't get me wrong – it often looks the same. Otium.

YOUNGER BROTHER. One to one they're ok.

MAN. But get them together and it's like a gang of crows – no group discipline. All they can say is 'Fuck this and fuck that.' Go to the can and it's still 'Snort this and shag that.' It's cool to slag off everything, see?

YOUNGER BROTHER. You don't know that when you're in it. Took me getting wed to see it proper – you need distance – a fresh stretch.

MAN. Know what they sound like when you open the bar door? Like someone's pulled the chain in an old toilet. Words pouring out their pipes. A bog cacophony. 'Spicy chicken pieces.' 'The Great Wall at Simatia.'

YOUNGER BROTHER. 'Jackson Pollock.'

MAN. 'The flowerbeds round Chaoyang district.' 'The Chinese economy.' Must be music to somebody's ears. We're on different planets. White banana trash, yellow on the outside.

Know what I'm saying? My head may be empty most of the time, but at least there's some space left up here. Their heads are like their fancy flats – crammed full of tack: Qing dynasty chairs, Tibetan masks, sandalwood boxes. A wee scattering of silk Tang poetry cushions. Everything's pirated. Mini terracotta warriors in their loos. Like they need to prove they're in China. I can't believe I used to respect – actually envy these people.

YOUNGER BROTHER. You were infatuated. For years. I remember . . . at home you used to try and eat Mum's dumplings with a knife and fork.

MAN. Did I? Really? A knife and fork?

YOUNGER BROTHER. A knife and fork. Special dumplings. For the would-be author.

MAN. Remember . . . what's his face . . . on the tenth floor? The guy with the fringe that stood up like wild straw?

YOUNGER BROTHER. Used to go to the shops on a motor-tricycle – like one of the last peasants – him?

MAN. Yeah. When he went abroad in '94 he didn't even know how to switch on a computer. Now he works in Silicon Valley. Got an MA grant paid for by Uncle Sam. What's that say about America?

YOUNGER BROTHER. Hey – it must be on the slide – if US prestige depends on importing cretins like him.

MAN. Not one of the Yanks I've met has been remotely interesting.

YOUNGER BROTHER. But our French friend, he was quite cool.

MAN. You think so? I thought he was a bit of a peasant actually. I used to say that to him – 'You're no jet-set international worker. You're a peasant. I can smell the kack.' He didn't disagree. Traffic lights weren't installed in his home town until the start of the eighties. He took his wee brother to see them. He told me, his little brother was gob-smacked, pointing his finger at the lights. 'Robots,' he says,

'Robots.' Frenchie said he just had to leave that town, he just had to get out. Did I tell you, one day I bumped into him and he was reeking. I just managed to get him out the door before the bouncers bashed him. We sat on the kerb. His white shirt was dirty, buttons popped. He always had three different coloured pens in his shirt pocket. You notice that?

YOUNGER BROTHER. Never did – naw.

MAN. He declared one was for writing down what his Chinese clients said. Green was for his American boss and blue was for what he thought himself. You know the joke about the pen mender?

YOUNGER BROTHER. No.

MAN. What are you if you have one pen in your shirt pocket? A high-school student. If you have two? A university student. If you have three? Then you're a pen mender.

YOUNGER BROTHER. He told me he was from Paris.

MAN. He went to uni in Paris, he wasn't from Paris. That's what I'm saying, he was from the French version of Anhui. He didn't mean to lie. He'd just forgotten the truth. See, at uni he hung out with the 'cool crowd'. He studied revolutions. The Chinese revolution, the French revolution, the American revolution. His chums were all lefties with rich mums and dads. So after graduation they walked into jobs in Daddy's firm or went globetrotting. He was the only one that had to find his own job. He was saying he forgot at university he was living in a capitalist country. That's what he says, sitting on the kerb, smelling of booze. Wouldn't stop talking. He said, 'Do you think I'm "super stupide"? I don't know why I'm here. I should have just studied Business, or Accountancy or Banking.' He started to blubber but no tears came, just this scraping sound in his throat. Going on about capitalism. He made no sense. I started to laugh. Him going on and on about capitalism was something to laugh about, right? Then this red Cherokee Jeep came along and shone its lights right at him. He fell back onto me, he looked like a frightened rabbit. I pushed him off in case somebody got the wrong idea. But then I felt something wobble in here. (*Points to his chest.*) Sort of . . . sick. I got him into a taxi. The whole way back to his place the taxi went through every single red light. Frenchie became quieter and quieter, then he suddenly pipes up. He's going on about how he was a grape someone had stood on. Then he says, 'You like books, don't you? I've got stacks. You can have them all.' 'Don't you have the time to read them?' I asks. 'Plenty time,' he says. 'But I'm going away and I'm not coming back.' 'But they're foreign books – I won't understand them.' 'In that case,' he smiles, 'use them as fuckin door-stoppers.' And then he starts laughing just like an hour ago I laughed in his face.

YOUNGER BROTHER. Why did he tell you all that for?

MAN. He was lonely. Disappointed.

Did you ever clock his hairstyle? Must have cost soup bones. He cut it on purpose before he came to China. He called it his Caesar-style. Veni, Vidi, Vici.

YOUNGER BROTHER. What's that mean?

MAN. It's Latin: 'I came, I saw, I conquered.' He never sussed in this world there's nowhere left to conquer.

In the end what's the difference between him and the foreigners who leave once they make their pile. If somebody told me the way forward was even darker I'd stay put in this alleyway – no going back, no way forward. Sometimes you know what's wrong, but you still don't know what to do about it.

YOUNGER BROTHER. I think Frenchie was great, only relying on himself . . . Are you afraid of dying?

MAN. No.

YOUNGER BROTHER. What are you scared of?

MAN. I'm scared of what the world is really like.

YOUNGER BROTHER. You believe in plenty good things.

MAN. Only sometimes.

Pause.

YOUNGER BROTHER. I admire you. I really do. You throw yourself right into things. You do what you want to. Stuff the consequences and what other people think. You know how to live. Me, what have I ever done? Like Dad says, I'm just ordinary . . . nothing to sing about.

MAN. You shouldn't listen to everything he says. You're well on the way.

Manager of the month, eh? Several times over. Top of the range motor. Nice house. Pretty wife. You've got AirMiles. What have I got? I would like some ordinary please.

YOUNGER BROTHER. No, you don't. Gran always says, the day you were born, the family got lucky.

MAN. Changed the Feng Shui? Huh! I'm half a barrel of rainwater. No, it's over. I'm going to look for another job. Start again.

YOUNGER BROTHER. Your boss will be years younger than you.

MAN. So what?

YOUNGER BROTHER. You think you can handle that?

MAN. So there's no way out? I'm stuck where I am?

YOUNGER BROTHER. Just keep on writing. Look, here's some money – take it. Her parents are coming down to stay for a break. Otherwise you could have had the spare room.

MAN. I'll get sorted. I checked my bank balance yesterday. There wasn't enough for a deposit. So this is . . . handy.

YOUNGER BROTHER. What do you expect? You drift along. (*Referring to the money.*) Put that in your pouch. I hope it's enough?

MAN. Ta.

YOUNGER BROTHER. I know how hard it is – you get used to a certain standard of living.

MAN. Let's go.

YOUNGER BROTHER. Shall we bother? (*Looks at his watch.*)

MAN. I've got stuff to shift tomorrow. Packing.

YOUNGER BROTHER. Keep your mind focused – or you'll never leave.

MAN. I know.

YOUNGER BROTHER. Want to go for a spin? (*Car keys.*)

MAN. Naw. I'm going to walk on a little further.

YOUNGER BROTHER. I'll give you a call.

MAN. Yeah – bye. (*Goes a few steps then stops.*) Hey, hey. Young brother? Kid? Daft question. Who is your favourite painter?

YOUNGER BROTHER. My favourite painter?

MAN. Aye. Off the top of your head.

YOUNGER BROTHER. Off the top of my head – if I had to pick one . . . (*Shrugs his shoulders.*) I think . . . Van Gogh.

MAN. Bring up your kid to be like him.

YOUNGER BROTHER. Thanks . . . I think.

MAN *exits.* YOUNGER BROTHER *looks a little weary.*

Scene Eleven

WOMAN *and* WIFE *waiting for the lift in* WIFE*'s apartment block.*

WOMAN. What are you thinking of?

WIFE. Those trousers, mmm.

WOMAN. The green ones – in Esprit?

WIFE. Mmm. Dream shop.

WOMAN. Very expensive.

WIFE. Everything in Esprit is big bucks. I was hesitating.
Should I buy them or not, should I? They'd go against my
cherry-perfect look, eh? Too 'career woman'. No, no, I've
made up my mind. I'm buying them first thing tomorrow.
Must have.

WOMAN. So is that your husband's only charm – his salary
and monthly bonus?

WIFE. So what?

WOMAN. Is it a reason to get married?

WIFE. How can you talk like you're seventy-two? You're
pathetic.

WOMAN. Is it old fashioned now to marry for love?

WIFE. Money makes you feel better. Tell me who do I hate?
Nobody. The have-nots, they know how to hate – proper
detest that doesn't stop like their boring grind doesn't stop.
When I was small we had nothing. I remember the Spring
Festival, it was live on TV. We didn't have a telly. I begged
Mum to let me go to my uncle's to watch it. I was only
little. But she kept saying no. 'Money's tight,' she said. No
bus fare. I don't know how long I argued. My dad's pal
joked, 'You'll get to see it tomorrow on the street corner
when folks talk about it.' I don't remember if she relented.
What I won't forget is shame in the dump, that feeling? The
threadbare carpet was like a trophy to my mum. For visitors
only. I don't want that for my kid.

WOMAN. It won't happen.

WIFE. Now, he works so hard. Leaves dead early and comes
back late. He's too tired to talk. He hits the sack right after
he's bolted his tea. Last night I sat next to him to watch his
face and he kicked me. He has bad dreams. It hurt so much
I kicked him back. Then he punched me, so I shook him
awake: 'Why did you punch me?' He was gasping, 'I was
fighting a bogey, ugly monster. Shouting on it to "fly, fly
away", and it leapt on top of my computer. When you were
shaking me it was like it had flown back onto me and
wasn't letting go!' He was so funny. I laughed till tears were

running down my face. How can a baby like that be a dad?
You know what he said next? I really love him for it. He
was lying there in his sweat, staring at the ceiling. I could
feel his heart beating beneath my hand.

WOMAN. What?

WIFE. 'I earn money to take care of you – the want can never
hurt you again. And if . . . if anything happens to me you'll
be well sorted.'

Why was he dreaming of a monster? Most likely cos I put
him under too much pressure.

WOMAN. Stop buying so many useless things.

WIFE. Why do I only think of shops? I'm obsessed. I'm in a
shop and I feel like I belong. I'm totally at home. People
don't realise comfortable is such an intense thrill. The till
and card swipe is so beautiful. Money can't buy you
happiness but without it you feel there is no chance. I don't
know – I must be bored. I must be.

WOMAN. Very much so.

WIFE. I got pregnant on purpose. I was scared of losing him.
He won't like me if I just sit around . . . between sprees.

WOMAN. You're on the same level. You're both a couple of
kids. He seems to like you well enough.

WIFE. When you two broke up I was scared cos your ex is like
me. Wasted time and pottering, wondering if there's
anything meaningful to do today.

WOMAN. That's not why we broke up. It's cos for the last
year solid all we've done is cheat. When I say cheat I'm not
talking about our dead-end affairs but how we gave
ourselves phoney hopes about our lives and who we were.
It's easy to use love and pretend.

The lift doors open.

Don't lose him by making the wrong decision.

WIFE. Will you be ok . . . on your own?

WOMAN. I'm old enough to take care of myself. You've got stuff to sort out yourselves.

WIFE. You too. We're mates, so I wish you both well. I'm happy when my friends are happy.

WOMAN. There's no hope for us. Love him and he thinks you're a bore. That's how he thinks . . . You're artless and dim to love somebody.

WIFE. When you live with someone you should try and give each other little surprises.

The lift doors close.

Scene Twelve

WOMAN *and* YOUNGER BROTHER *stand on opposite sides of the stage facing each other. When they move they do so as if shouldering a heavy weight. They are shadows dragged along by car headlights.*

MAN *and* WIFE *stand in a white light. They are standing facing each other with a bathroom mirror which doesn't exist in-between. They are inspecting themselves.* MAN *blinks, pouts, grinds his teeth, and smiles then laughs, then carefully looks himself over in the mirror, as if looking for the stranger inside himself.* WIFE *uses both her hands to slowly massage her forehead, eyes and cheeks. She is counting to herself: 1, 2, 3, 4. She is gazing into the distance with deep longing and she smiles wryly as she applies her face cream, drop by drop.* MAN *becomes still, his face is expressionless. He lifts his toothbrush and then puts it down again.*

WIFE *turns off the light.*

Scene Thirteen

In the WOMAN's *flat. The* MAN *is looking for a bottle of paracetamol.* WOMAN *appears behind him.*

MAN (*startled*). Don't do that. I nearly had a heart attack.

WOMAN. I didn't think there was anybody in.

MAN. Of course you didn't.

WOMAN. I should have rang the bell.

MAN. Skip the dizzy act.

WOMAN. I said I didn't know anybody was . . . home.

MAN. What are you back for? Is Mister IT away on business?

WOMAN. You've been drinking. I can smell it.

MAN. Do you think I've had too much to drink?

WOMAN. Haven't you been writing?

MAN. No, not a stroke – thanks for your interest. Much appreciated. Don't turn the light on. It's too bright, my head's splitting.

WOMAN. I'll turn the bathroom light on. (*Turns on the bathroom light.*)

MAN. Have you seen the paracetamol? I can't find it.

WOMAN. I . . . I took them to the office.

MAN. Did you . . . really?

WOMAN. It's not what you think.

MAN. You know I get migraines.

WOMAN. I thought . . .

MAN. You thought . . . you thought. Don't I look like a grown-up? My head's been pounding all day, nonstop. Starts behind my eyes. I'd drill a hole in my skull if there was a drill handy. No, no, don't touch me. (*Picks up a packet of cigarettes, pauses, takes one.*) Want one?

WOMAN. No. I'm fagged out. Cocktails with –

MAN. I know you have. You'll be glad – I found a place to stay.

WOMAN. Where did you get the money?

MAN. Why do you need to know?

WOMAN. Your younger brother. I already said you can stay here for a while.

MAN. I've got a hunch that wouldn't go down well with your future husband. Just a hunch. Gag on his cyber sandwich if he heard you say that. No thanks.

WOMAN. We've already discussed it.

MAN. Oh aye. What's it got to do with him? It's your place and our botch. Our special botch. A wonderful hash, unique to us. It's ours. Nobody else's. Nobody could have done it in the same way – in the style of. So you can tell him to keep his nose out. And by the way, what's this sneaking in and out for? You want your toothbrush, your dental floss, just come in and take it.

WOMAN. I saw her this evening. Looking very winsome . . .

MAN. Who?

WOMAN. . . . like lady drunks often are. Soaking up a few voddies and draped all over a right horse's head.

MAN. Huh?

WOMAN. Your girlfriend. Your French instructor.

MAN. Oh, I see. You obviously don't know she's planning on starting an import/export business. Yeah. She wants to relocate. Export herself abroad with the foreign gent. I introduced her. Gave her a leg up, so to speak. Helping fulfil a person's wishes – I'm like that. Don't say I didn't do the same for you. I mean, see me, see wishes.

WOMAN. When did you split up with her? You never said.

MAN. What? So that must mean you never read the whole of the diary. You should have read on, turnt a few more pages,

it was all there, I assure you. Times, dates. Horse's head
flashing his wad at her.

Did you rush over this time of night just to tell me that? You
think you can just walk in . . . just fuckin breeze right in.
Don't think I'm going to forget.

WOMAN. It wasn't meant bad – I just wanted to know where I
stood.

MAN. It's got nothing to do with you.

WOMAN. Not now.

MAN. Is there a word for someone who can fake their feelings,
even their thinking? (*He lies on the sofa.*) I'm tired.

WOMAN. Shall I close the door? (*The bathroom door, which
is letting in light.*) I want to listen to some music?

MAN. Whatever.

WOMAN. I'll keep it down.

MAN. Just don't put on any piano stuff. Not right now –
please.

WOMAN *changes her choice of CD.* MAN *changes
position. The music comes on. It's an '80s love song. The
song makes her feel sad. She walks towards the* MAN.

WOMAN. Is it ok? The volume? (*The* MAN *has his back to
her.*) You'll get a chill sleeping like that.

MAN. Turn off the air-conditioning then.

He turns to face her. She is standing over him.

What are you standing there for?

WOMAN. No reason. Just looking at you.

MAN. Well, do you mind? You're making me nervous.

The WOMAN *lies down on the sofa beside the* MAN. *A
kind of mild slow struggle ensues as she tries to hit him and
he blocks her moves.*

What are you doing?

WOMAN (*takes his hand and examines it*). You've got beautiful fingers, a writer's hands.

MAN. That's cos I am a writer.

WOMAN (*listens to his chest*). Your heartbeat is like an old man's.

MAN. Everything's old. Everything's dodgy. Lungs. Kidneys.

WOMAN. Such a clever . . . clever brain.

MAN. Not any more. When I was young – yeah.

WOMAN. Smart man.

MAN. I was like a bird. Nothing out of reach. But that's all done and dusted.

WOMAN. You know the story of the very intelligent kid and the old scholar who couldn't abide him? Do you? The old scholar says, 'You might be clever now but it's no guarantee you'll be clever when you're old.' And the boy gibes, 'Well, you must have been awfully clever when you were younger, Mister.' (*Long pause.*) What's going to happen to us?

MAN. Nothing. Things don't change just like that.

WOMAN. I'm the girlfriend you lived with the longest.

MAN. Yes.

WOMAN. You said you needed me. You promised to marry me.

MAN. I promised too many things.

WOMAN. You say things without seeing the outcome. You said we would get married and have kids after I gave up smoking. It sounded so regular and nice. I gave up fags. Two whole years I was gasping – never had a puff. Our first time . . . remember . . . ?

MAN. Let's not talk about this now, ok?

WOMAN. When I fell pregnant the first time I was still officially somebody else's girlfriend.

MAN. Where's this getting us?

WOMAN. He'd already bought me the ring. He was a sweet man. I won't see you any more, not after tonight.

MAN. I know.

WOMAN. Tomorrow everything will change cos you won't be around. In three years with you, know what I learnt? I learnt to cheat myself, to excuse myself, to pretend. That's how a person becomes dead-end, don't you think? A pretend woman. Even though I was a complete fake I always knew there was someone better inside me . . . someone that I dare not be or even wish for. I trashed the life I could have had. He bought me a ring. I never knew how good it was. I never knew.

MAN. You can go back.

WOMAN. How can I go back? I won't bump into him again. And you won't even miss me. Will you? I feel such a clown the way I relied on you for so long.

MAN. It wasn't all like that. I loved you too.

WOMAN. Why didn't we make a go of it?

MAN. I don't know . . . I couldn't say.

They hug, and try to separate, get entangled in each other, or are unable to move as if to confirm the distance between them and their separation.

It's too hot.

WOMAN. Are you feeling alright?

MAN. Nothing's wrong with me. Look, nothing's changed – you know that. You want to recycle all that rubbish again? We'd just . . . in the bedroom, then you'd cry, then in the morning, slamming doors. But maybe that's what you came round for? One last bash?

WOMAN. That is not what I want.

MAN. What do you want? Do you know? Your body says one thing – your head something different altogether. I know you can't stand me touching you. It's him, you want him, so why don't you just . . . go.

WOMAN. Look around you, see whose flat you're in – don't tell me to go anywhere.

MAN. Wow – I'm impressed. Your anger-management course is really kicking in – stick at it.

WOMAN. Fuck you.

MAN. Women, where'd they come from?

WOMAN. If I was you I wouldn't worry about where 'women come from' but where you're going to go next.

MAN. Is that right?

WOMAN. Yes. Your life's a shambles.

MAN. Could you turn off that stupid music toy!

She emphatically stays where she is. He gets up and turns off the CD player, then returns to lying on the sofa.

That's another of your defining habits – using the repeat key on the CD. You'd think after all this time I'd have made a dent. Made a few adjustments. A person's habits are hard to change. But see that? (*Points to silent CD.*) That's your last lesson.

He turns his back to her on the sofa. WOMAN sits lost in thought. She is angry. She presses her fingers against her temples. Stands with her eyes shut. Sits, opens her eyes. Then stands again with her eyes shut. She walks past where he is lying. He turns on the sofa.

(*Guardedly.*) What are you up to now?

WOMAN. I'm not up to anything. I'm going to get a glass of water.

He watches her leave, then slips from the sofa, moving close to the kitchen. He picks up a few books, and then remembers something. Then as if he's heard something from the kitchen he rushes offstage. We hear the sound of a door being opened.

Scene Fourteen

WIFE *enters her living room from the bedroom. She switches on the TV. The sound suddenly drops in volume.* YOUNGER BROTHER *enters in his pyjamas.*

YOUNGER BROTHER. What time's it? Haven't you been to bed yet?

WIFE. I couldn't sleep. You pushed me out the bed. Kicking as usual. You must be dreaming football or something. Go back to bed.

YOUNGER BROTHER. I can hear the telly. It's ok – you don't need to turn it down.

WIFE. What time did you get in from work?

YOUNGER BROTHER. Well after one.

WIFE. Overtime still?

YOUNGER BROTHER. We're planning the ten-year schedule for the office. Do you know what you're going to be doing in ten years' time? Does anybody?

WIFE. No. I haven't a clue what I'm doing tomorrow.

YOUNGER BROTHER. We've been working on it solid – all week. The deadline is due in . . . (*Looks at his wristwatch.*) nine-and-a-half hours . . . I think I'll go back to my kip.

WIFE. Do you notice when I go out? Do I wake you?

YOUNGER BROTHER. No.

WIFE. When I come in?

YOUNGER BROTHER. Yeah. When you come in, all I hear is wobbly heels . . . clickety clackety.

WIFE. Come here, hon, you are sweet.

YOUNGER BROTHER *sleepily embraces* WIFE.

What were you dreaming about? You are hot.

YOUNGER BROTHER. I was dreaming about a tea bush. Not football. A nice bright green tea bush.

WIFE. You must be thirsty. Darling?

YOUNGER BROTHER. Mmm.

WIFE. I love you.

They sway together, it develops into a lazy sort of dance.

YOUNGER BROTHER (*head resting on her shoulder, almost sleeping*). What's that smell? It smells good.

WIFE. Shiseido – you like it?

YOUNGER BROTHER (*still with his eyes shut*). How much do you weigh?

WIFE. 50 kilos. Why?

YOUNGER BROTHER. The company wants to put you on the family health scheme. I have to put your weight on the form. If you want to have the baby I can put it down too – all together, eh?

WIFE. I'll seem even more of a housewife then.

YOUNGER BROTHER. Let's have the baby . . . it will be around to look after us when we're old.

WIFE. Isn't the package you're earning enough for our pension plan?

YOUNGER BROTHER. I earn plenty. Share options and high-interest package. Big bucks trussed up in offshore account. Well sussed.

WIFE. Isn't it dangerous to be so well off? Somebody might try and kill us, like on TV.

YOUNGER BROTHER. Don't be silly. What I'm saying is, if we don't have a kid, there'll be nobody to look after us when we're old.

WIFE. I'll look after you.

YOUNGER BROTHER. You'll be old too. You're two years older than me, mind. But think about it – when we're sitting

in our day chairs who's going to visit and prom-walk us?
Nobody.

WIFE. We've got friends.

YOUNGER BROTHER. Our friends will be old too. Look at
Gran. She lies in bed, day and night. My brother asked her
once, 'Do you think there's a point to living?' Gran replied:
'A person's life is dawn then dusk.' That's her attitude. My
brother goes round a lot. If she didn't have us, think how
lonely she'd be. Everybody lives longer nowadays. We have
to think about these things.

WIFE. Let's have dimple chin then. But let's have more than
one.

YOUNGER BROTHER. When Mum had me she was in labour
for fifteen hours. Then she wasn't best pleased that it was
another boy. A little runt at that. After that, I seemed to keep
on upsetting her. She had my brother to compare me with.
She'd look at his grades then mine. Even when I did well
there was always 'a big difference' between him and me.
Know what I mean?

WIFE. Do you hate her?

YOUNGER BROTHER. I don't think so. I dwelt on it too
much at the time. But I'm better off than him now. I have
you. He didn't say it but I know he envies us.

WIFE. You were with him earlier – and you gave him money?

YOUNGER BROTHER. Are you angry? (WIFE *shakes her
head*.) Thanks, wife.

*He caresses her cheek. They end up sitting watching the
mute TV.*

WIFE. What did you talk about?

YOUNGER BROTHER. We drank. I can't really remember.
He was upset about something. He was talking nonsense.
He's in a muddle. Who can guess what somebody who
wants to be a writer is thinking? Three years ago he had
a decent salary. He doesn't think normal. His brain works
in a different way.

WIFE. Will he get famous – you know, as a writer?

YOUNGER BROTHER. I don't know if he can even survive. It's hard. To think I wanted to be a painter, studied colours and all. I'd miss my telly ads too much, eh?

WIFE. You are much more realistic than him.

YOUNGER BROTHER. What do you mean? That I don't have any ideals or what?

WIFE. Ok – tell me why people always put youth on some sort of pedestal?

YOUNGER BROTHER. What are you talking about? I'll never get back to sleep now.

Pause.

You know, I never noticed before how in soaps there's always stuff about the legal system? How no one gets away with being a baddie? You noticed that?

WIFE. Why don't I want to go back to work, huh?

YOUNGER BROTHER. You look after this family. That's a job.

WIFE. But sometimes I'm afraid of being at home by myself. I think nonsense. Wacky stuff. Aren't you worried I'll go crazy on my own all day?

YOUNGER BROTHER. Don't be silly . . . Do you . . . do you still scream when you wash my shirts?

WIFE. No.

YOUNGER BROTHER. I heard you, from outside on the landing. Last week there.

WIFE. I was polishing the floor, husband. I'd just put some buff down and out skittered two cockroaches . . . At least they've chased away the red ants.

YOUNGER BROTHER. They bite . . .

WIFE. Let's meet at the mall tomorrow. We can go shopping together.

YOUNGER BROTHER. Ok. (*He yawns.*)

WIFE. Why is it the moment I mention shopping you yawn?

YOUNGER BROTHER. I'm tired. Come on, let's get some sleep. I need some kip.

They rise.

Hit the sack and guaranteed the alarm's off.

They hug and separate as before.

Scene Fifteen

In the WOMAN'*s flat.* WOMAN *enters from the kitchen with a glass of water in her hand. There is a small superficial scratch above her wrist. The* MAN *follows, he is holding a small kitchen knife.*

WOMAN. Do you think my memory's that bad?

MAN. I know you. I'll always be able to hurt you, won't I? Did so then.

WOMAN. In my whole life that really was the dumbest thing I've ever done.

MAN. Oh, you were just tinkering with it this time? Can I take it away now?

WOMAN. No. There's still some of my blood on it. I should keep it. I just wanted to scare you.

MAN. You're spiteful, aren't you?

WOMAN. But you're not worth dying for.

WOMAN *sits down.* MAN *holds the knife under the light, peering at a line of script on the cutting edge of the blade.*

MAN. There's plenty I suppose I won't be forgiven. Was that the worst I did – when you cut yourself?

WOMAN. No, you were smoking once and you set fire to my fucking hair.

MAN. So I did. Sorry.

WOMAN. Put it away. You might get to like it. Does it make you feel tough?

MAN. You keep it – since you care about your possessions so much. (*Looking away from* WOMAN, *gives her the knife.*) Let me have a look at your wrist.

WOMAN. There's nothing there – you can hardly see it.

MAN. I'm going to go when it gets light – first bus. Ok?

WOMAN. Ok. (*Referring to the bulging holdall.*) Will you get everything in there?

MAN. I've hardly anything left here. You won't have anything left soon yourself . . . Bare flat, blank canvas, eh? You know, I still don't get it – why do you want to marry that guy?

WOMAN. What's the point in wasting time with you? Zero affection. Zero money. It's a pure dead end. I'm nearly thirty-two.

MAN. Hey, you're making this easy. It's amazing how you don't really know people. I've never heard you . . . talk like that. Fondle bucks. You've turned into one of them. But I'm easy, I'll get over it. By the way, I'll pay you back . . . what I owe you . . . once I get sorted.

WOMAN. Do you know what self-respect is? I never counted on you repaying me anything. Not ever. Sometimes I don't remember anything at all 'cept the disappointments. I don't have any more time for you. You can shove it. (*He makes to reply.*) Don't say another word. Mind your books. I'm sure you'll find them really really useful! You don't want to disappoint people, they're starving to read you.

MAN. I hate to tell you this but see, when I write you are definitely not my audience.

WOMAN. Fine – smashing news.

MAN. Just cos you never got what you wanted doesn't mean I'm unable to give it, or couldn't give it, if I was so inclined. I don't know how to put this but some ladies, no matter how long they hang around, are only ever sort of transitions in an artist's life – passing through, see?

WOMAN. You think you're a real artist? You make me ill. Who knows you're a writer, apart from me, your brother and oh – your mother? You blow your own trumpet. Where's this big novel you're writing? I haven't seen it. Let's play 'Hunt the Masterpiece'. The only thing that proves you write is that stupid diary.

MAN. You think so?

WOMAN. You really took me in – like you conned everybody else.

MAN. You feel conned? Maybe that's cos you're a pretentious arty-farty. You go to openings – yeah, for the free booze. It's all a tin of shit to you. It gave you a bit of glitz going with a writer. But posers are feeble. They have no future cos their grasp on the present is so weak. They crave being attractive – who's in, who's out. Who makes them look good. If I'm successful or not, your . . . stamp will be totally . . . absent. I wouldn't let you read a thing I wrote – you couldn't muster an original opinion on anything. You're polite and you're nice, as a vassal kingdom. And that's about it. 'Nough said?

MAN *gets up to pack his things.* WOMAN *sits gripping the knife in her hand.*

WOMAN. I swear . . . I really hate you.

MAN. Hatred is not a good emotion. Do you remember how we first met? Louis, the French dude – I've finally remembered his real name. One evening we're playing pool and you swan in on your lonesome. Louis clocks you right away. 'When you need a babe,' he says, 'you can't find a single one. Then when you don't, they're all over the shop. She's tasty.' That was his spiel. I remember my reply: 'She's game enough – wearing a low-cut dress, with a chest that flat.' My brother shouted you over, he recognised you – you worked in the next block. 'Fancy a game, doubles?' But you knocked him back. He said, 'What? You scared to let it all hang out?' I said, 'What's all there to hang out?' Bit of cheek. You didn't mind. In fact you were laughing with Louis. Do I need to finish? Do you think we ever moved on from that? I don't think so. A bit of self-deception goes a long way.

WOMAN. Speak for yourself.

MAN. You don't get it? Well, it's not an exact science – words. You can't make me make sense. The world and me, we're strangers. And, I guarantee, I hate myself more than you ever could. (*Lights a cigarette – puts it out.*) Did you know, Louis is dead?

WOMAN. People die every day.

MAN. He liked you. Don't you feel sad? He used to call you 'baby-sweet', didn't he? What a dingle. He didn't see wrong about one thing. When he said you were tasty. 'Stick with her,' he said. 'She smells of fresh notes, she's minted. Check the power dress.'

WOMAN. Fuck off. You bastard. Don't think you can tell me who I am. I'll tell you something, I drank a lot that night and when I woke up the next day, your back was to me and I had no idea at all who you were.

They are silent for a long while.

MAN. Really?

WOMAN. Really.

MAN *stands reluctantly, zips his holdall, puts on his jacket. The* WOMAN *picks up the knife. She holds it limply.*

MAN. Some people live on memories. But for us? There's nothing there. It's better if we both forget.

WOMAN. You forced me to talk like this. You made me. It wasn't all bad. I wanted to live with you. Us.

MAN. Same here.

WOMAN. I wanted you. I wanted to own you. I didn't know how to love you. I couldn't find a reason for loving you, which made me want to love you even more. How I felt wasn't warranted by anything you did.

Once, one evening when I was out on the balcony watching
out or you, I was kicking heels sort of and knocked my shoe
off accidentally. It fell sixteen floors. I looked and saw it
and then I couldn't see it. I ran down with a torch and
looked for it amongst the bicycles. There were too many –
I couldn't find it. You bought me those shoes. They were a
present.

MAN. It doesn't matter.

WOMAN. I sat over there, you took them out the box – put
them on my feet.

MAN. I know. I lived with you.

WOMAN. You don't want to go, do you?

MAN. But you don't want me to stay.

*Goes to his holdall at the door and shoulders it. Turns back
before he leaves.*

I want to wish you both good fortune.

WOMAN. You? Why say that?

MAN. People should wish each other good luck. I really mean
it – no edge.

WOMAN *disappears from the light.*

Scene Sixteen

MAN. Other people might not notice the lines round her
eyes, eh? She still looks so refined in soft light. Who was
she? What has she become? I don't know. All I know is a
woman . . . is gone. Taxi! She won't look back. She'll not
be watching me from the balcony. She's already got a new
home, a new life, a new future. She has already left and is
past regretting what we don't have. Something about her
made me feel small. Her affair with that guy was like my
own shadow. When I resigned I had confidence, thumbs up,
but her and him slowly ate away at all that. Made me pity

myself. Now every step feels like I'm walking a little
further into middle age. When the taxi gets to The Lama
Temple, the view over Yonghegong Bridge will be sunrise.
The sun will show her beauty. An orange glow filtered
through carbon dioxide, nitrogen dioxide, particles; a
fluorescent tube. I don't know how long in this city the
sun has only been able to shine as bright as a factory bulb.
A Xerox of daylight. I suddenly feel before me it is raining
all over the city.

He is crying.

The End.

A Nick Hern Book

In the Bag first published in Great Britain as a paperback original in 2005 by Nick Hern Books Limited, 14 Larden Road, London W3 7ST in association with the Traverse Theatre, Edinburgh

Cover image: Laurence Winram

Typeset by Country Setting, Kingsdown, Kent CT14 8ES
Printed and bound in Great Britain by Cox and Wyman Limited, Reading, Berks

A CIP catalogue record for this book is available from the British Library

ISBN 1 85459 874 0